TEACHING SECONDARY
ENGLISH
General Editor: Peter King

DRAMA IN THE
ENGLISH CLASSROOM

Also in this series

ENCOURAGING TALK
Lewis Knowles

ENCOUNTERS WITH BOOKS
Teaching fiction 11–16
David Jackson

ENCOURAGING WRITING
Robert Protherough

TEACHING THE BASIC SKILLS
Spelling, punctuation and grammar in secondary English
Don Smedley

POETRY EXPERIENCE
Stephen Tunnicliffe

MARKING AND ASSESSMENT IN ENGLISH
Pauline Chater

USING COMPUTERS IN ENGLISH
A practical guide
Phil Moore

DRAMA IN THE ENGLISH CLASSROOM

KEN BYRON

London   METHUEN   *New York*

First published in 1986 by
Methuen & Co. Ltd
11 New Fetter Lane, London EC4P 4EE

Published in the USA by
Methuen & Co.
in association with Methuen, Inc.
29 West 35th Street, New York NY 10001

© 1986 Ken Byron

Photoset by
Rowland Phototypesetting Ltd
Bury St Edmunds, Suffolk
Printed in Great Britain by
Richard Clay, The Chaucer Press,
Bungay, Suffolk

British Library Cataloguing in
Publication Data

Byron, Ken
Drama in the English classroom. –
(Teaching secondary English)
1. Drama – Study and teaching
(Secondary) – Great Britain
I. Title   II. Series
792'.07'12   PN1701

ISBN 0-416-38030-1
ISBN 0-416-38040-9 Pbk

Library of Congress Cataloging in
Publication Data

Byron, Ken, 1927–
Drama in the English classroom.
(Teaching secondary English)
Bibliography: P.
1. Drama in education.
I. Title.   II. Series.
PN3171.B97   1986   371.3'32
86-8539

ISBN 0-416-38030-1
ISBN 0-416-38040-9 (Pbk.)

CONTENTS

Acknowledgements p. ix

General editor's preface p. xi

1 WHAT KIND OF BOOK IS THIS? *p.* 1

Strand one – the journal p. 2; Strand two – purposes, strategies and evaluation p. 4; Weaving the strands p. 4; Omissions p. 5; What is the best way to use the book? p. 6

2 JOURNAL ONE: DRAGON SLAYER *p.* 7

Drama as a 'way in' to narrative text
Some functions of teacher role
Language opportunities
Some aspects of pupil role
Materials and space
Still image (waxworks)

3 SOME ASSUMPTIONS *p.* 19

4 JOURNAL TWO: 'THE WAY WEST' *p.* 24

Working from a theme – 'Wagon Train'
How to plan and yet be open to children's ideas
Building belief and seriousness in drama

Phase one: building the context p. 26; *Phase two: building an
identity p.* 29; *Phase three: the meeting p.* 31;
Maggie's response to my notes p. 33

5 HOW IS A DRAMA LESSON PLANNED AND
CARRIED OUT? *p.* 41

Enquiry and Definition p. 43; *The drama p.* 53;
Notes p. 58

6 JOURNAL THREE: LORD OF THE FLIES *p.* 59

Drama used in relation to narrative text
Teacher role
Opportunities for writing in role arising from the drama

7 DRAMA AND NARRATIVE FICTION *p.* 66

Similarities between drama and narrative fiction p. 67;
Difficulties in looking at a work of fiction p. 69; *Differences
between drama and narrative fiction p.* 72; *Strategies p.* 80;
Notes p. 85

8 WORKING ON PLAYTEXT *p.* 86

Phase one: the way in p. 87; *Phase two: working directly on
the text p.* 87; *Phase three: review p.* 88

9 JOURNAL FOUR: SMITH *p.* 90

Drama working broadly 'in parallel' with reading of
narrative text
Building belief through slow, careful elaboration of
dramatic context and role

Teacher role
Finding a direction 'within' the drama

10 JOURNAL FIVE: BEOWULF *p.* 105

Teacher role
Language possibilities
When and why to stop the drama
Finding a direction within the drama

11 DRAMA AND LANGUAGE *p.* 116

*Language development in a new context p. 117; Language
development through new role-relationships p. 118;
The 'reality' of the drama p. 125; Concreteness and
abstraction p. 127; Varieties of language development p. 132;
The quality of the drama p. 135; Notes p. 140*

12 JOURNAL SIX: FATHER AND DAUGHTER *p.* 141

Protection and risk in drama
Use of 'presentation' in drama
Demands of working with older pupils

13 DRAMA AND EVALUATION *p.* 153

*Trying to evaluate a drama is a bit like trying to evaluate a
party p. 153; Evaluation requires clarity about aims p. 154;
What kinds of learning are possible in drama? p. 156*

14 SOME RESOURCES *p.* 168

*General 'practical' books for the teacher p. 168; Manuals
p. 168; Going in deeper p. 169; Drama associations p. 169;
Drama journals p. 169; Resource packs p. 170*

Bibliography p. 171

Index p. 174

ACKNOWLEDGEMENTS

The author and publishers would like to thank the following for permission to reproduce extracts in this book: Megan Schaffner, 'Language development through drama' in *Drama, Language and Learning*, National Association for Drama in Education, Australia; Rosemary Sutcliff, *Dragon Slayer*, Penguin Books; Angela Wilson and Roy Cockcroft, *Some Uses of Role-Play as an Approach to the Study of Fiction*, Wakefield Literature and Learning Project.

I should also like to thank Peter King for his support and understanding during the writing of this book.

A special word of thanks goes to the teachers with whom I worked on the Advanced Diploma in Drama course at Leicester University. As the text makes clear, the book draws heavily on their experiences in using drama in the English classroom.

GENERAL EDITOR'S PREFACE

English remains a core subject in the secondary school curriculum as the confident words of a recent HMI document reveal:

> English is of vital importance in the development of pupils as individuals and as members of society: our language is our principal means of making sense of our experience and communication with others. The teaching of English is concerned with the essential skills of speech, reading and writing, and with literature. Schools will doubtless continue to give them high priority.
>
> (*The School Curriculum*, DES, 1981)

Such confidence belies the fact that there has been, and continues to be, much debate among practitioners as to exactly what constitutes English. If the desired consensus remains rather far off at least the interested teacher now has a large and useful literature on which he or she can profitably reflect in the attempt to answer the question 'What is English?' There have been notable books designed to reorientate teachers' thinking about the subject ranging from those absorbed by the necessary theoretical analysis, like John Dixon's *Growth Through English* (Oxford, rev. edn 1975), to those working outwards from new research into classroom language, like *From Communication to Curriculum*, by Douglas Barnes (Penguin, 1976); but there are not so many books intended to help teachers get a purchase on their day-to-day activities (a fine exception is *The English Department Handbook* recently published by the ILEA English Centre). To gain such a purchase requires confidence built not from making 'everything new' so much as learning to combine the best from the older traditions with some of those newer ideas. And preferably these ideas have to be seen to have emerged from effective classroom teaching. The English teacher's aims have to be continually reworked in the light of new experience, and the assurance necessary to manage this is bred out of the convictions of other experienced practitioners. This is of particular importance to the new and inexperienced teacher. It is to such teachers and student teachers that this series is primarily directed.

The books in this series are intended to give practical guidance in the various areas of the English curriculum. Each area is treated in a separate volume in order to gain the necessary space in which to discuss it at some length. The aim of the series is twofold: to describe good practice by exploring the approaches and activities reflected in the daily work of an English teacher in the comprehensive school; and to give a practical lead to teachers who wish to try out for themselves a wider repertoire of teaching skills and ways of organizing syllabuses and lessons. Taken as whole, the series does not press upon the reader a ready-made philosophy, but attempts to provide a map of the English teaching landscape in which the separate volumes highlight an individual feature of that terrain, representing its particular characteristics while reminding us of the continuity between these differing elements in the overall topography.

The series addresses itself to the 11–16 age range with an

additional volume on sixth-form work, and assumes a mixed ability grouping, at least in the first two years of schooling. Each volume begins with a discussion of the problems and rationale of its chosen aspect of English and goes on to describe practical ways in which the teachers can organize their syllabus and lessons to achieve their intended goals, and ends with a brief guide to books, resources, etc. The individual volumes are written by experienced teachers with a particular interest in their chosen area and the ideas they express have been proved by them or their colleagues in their own classrooms.

It is at the level of the practical that any synthesis of the various approaches to English can be gained, and to accomplish this every teacher must be in possession of a rationale and an awareness of good methods wherever and however they have been achieved. By reading the books in this series it is to be hoped that teachers will be encouraged to try out for themselves ideas found effective by their colleagues so gaining the confidence to make their own informed choice and planning in their own classrooms.

Peter King
July 1983

1
WHAT KIND OF BOOK
IS THIS?

When I was asked to write this book I spent a considerable amount of time thinking about what was the most appropriate form for it. The following considerations weighed heavily in my eventual decisions about its form. They are in no particular order.

- I wanted it to have the feel of the classroom about it – with as much as possible in the way of examples of interesting practice.
- These examples of practice should illustrate both the difficulties and the exciting possibilities of using drama in the English classroom.
- The book should as far as possible be written from the viewpoint of a teacher like those who will most probably use the book – interested and keen to begin to use drama (or to use it to greater effect) but by no means certain how to set about it.
- It should offer a clear theoretical base from which teachers can develop their work – in particular in terms of the

connections between the concerns of the English teacher
and the medium of drama.

- Although I wanted the book to offer teachers real practical
help with the 'how' as well as the 'why', I did not intend to
write a manual, with specific sample lessons for them to try
out. Rather, it seemed important to help teachers to an
understanding of how to construct their own work,
employing the plentiful material for drama which the rest of
their English work supplies.

- The book should be as varied in form and layout as possible
– including narrative and anecdote, charts and diagrams as
well as exposition and analysis. It seemed important, just as
in teaching, to find forms that both were appropriate to
my aims as teacher/writer and would offer varied 'ways in'
for learners/readers.

- I could not cover everything, therefore it was important to
provide references to allow readers to follow up ideas as
they might wish and need.

The form I finally settled on consisted of two broad strands,
which I have tried to weave together as carefully as possible.

Strand one – the journal

I have had the privilege recently of assisting a number of
English teachers, over a long period of time (two years) to start
or develop further the use of drama in their classrooms. We
have watched each other teach; planned, taught and post-
mortemed together; and spent a lot of hours in talk about a
variety of lessons and teaching projects. The journal is closely
based on their experiences and their attempts to come to terms
with the demands and opportunities of working in drama.

The 'writer' of the journal is a *fictional* English teacher – let
us call him Mike – intelligent, committed to teaching, several
years into his career and reasonably confident about what he is
doing as an English teacher, willing to experiment, but not

without concerns about control, security and structure. He is fictional, but all the work he records and comments on I have observed happening in classrooms, though it was taught by various teachers, and not one. Sometimes because of limitations of space I have compressed elements from two or even three lessons/projects by different people into one. Mike 'represents' the teachers I have worked with, and others like them – his struggles and excitements are theirs. He is a device, if you will, to try to compress a complex and challenging process of learning for a teacher into a few entries in a journal. Doubtless the compression will mean some oversimplification and crudity, but I felt it worth the attempt to try and write a large portion of the book directly from the viewpoint of a teacher who has the same interests and concerns as many of those who will read it.

Maggie, who also features in the journal, is a teacher of English, but experienced and confident in the use of drama. Not every teacher in Mike's position will have the help of a Maggie, although some will be able to gain support from a more experienced colleague, an adviser/advisory teacher or local drama teachers' association. Maggie is really another 'compression device'. She is there because her greater experience allows me to include more developed insights and analyses of the work than Mike could achieve, given the limitations of his experience of working in drama, particularly in the early stages. She had to be there to hasten his awareness, otherwise the journal would have had to be several times its present length!

Through the course of the journal, Mike develops in his understanding of, and capacity to use, drama – much as the teachers I worked with did. They needed at first to work in ways that gave them a reasonable degree of security and they needed to see clear benefits for their English work out of the drama from the beginning – so early work was often tied, say, to helping the children's understanding of a class reader. Then gradually, as they saw the benefits of drama *per se*, they would be more ready to broaden the range of purposes they were prepared to work for in drama.

I chose the journal form because it is one many teachers will be familiar with and because it offers the opportunity to use anecdote, narrative, comment and dialogue to convey the immediacy of the classroom encounter in a readable and unpretentious way. The reader will judge whether I have succeeded or not.

Strand two – purposes, strategies and evaluation

If part of my purpose is to examine the immediacy of the classroom encounter, another is to help readers stand back from the examples of practice offered, and from their own work, to ask a number of key questions:

1 What is the nature of drama and how does it work?
2 How does drama relate/contribute to my purposes as an English teacher?
3 What strategies can I employ and what difficulties am I likely to meet?
4 How do I evaluate what is going on in drama?

These are tackled in a series of chapters which operate mainly through conventional exposition, argument and analysis, though plentiful examples of practice are given to support and illustrate the argument.

Weaving the strands

The two strands are designed to be complementary, to tie together and support each other. I have tried to ensure that they do so in two ways:

1 Broadly speaking, related material in both strands is grouped together in the text. Thus, for example, the journal entries where drama is used in relation to a class reader are

mainly clustered around Chapter 7 on drama and narrative fiction.

2 I have employed a simple system of two-way cross-referencing between material in both strands, so that, for example, Chapter 11 on drama and language refers the reader to illustrative material in the journal. Where appropriate, journal entries carry references to those general chapters which amplify issues raised in that part of the journal.

Omissions

In a book of this length it is impossible to deal adequately with all the connections between English and drama. So, inevitably, there are omissions. There is, for example, nothing about drama and poetry in the pages that follow. I have opted to deal as adequately as possible with those areas – particularly narrative fiction and language development – which offer the most ready connections with drama, and on ways of making the connections that seemed to me most likely to get people started and to move them to a position of some familiarity and confidence with using drama processes in the English classroom. Once people get to that stage they should have no difficulty in devising their own approaches to other areas, such as poetry.

Playtext is not omitted, but is dealt with very briefly. I have been taken to task for this! It has been suggested to me that 'more could be made of "Drama and Playtext" as this is the area that all English teachers are directly concerned with. If they do no other drama in their work they have to consider playscripts.' My deliberate decision to put the main emphasis elsewhere stems from a fear that paying much attention to playtext would encourage people to limit their perceptions of the common ground between English and drama – 'playtext is where drama comes into English' – and to ignore the broader possibilities. In any case, in Chapter 7 I have dealt with approaches that can be used equally effectively on playtext. I think, too, that playtext is more complex to work at in the classroom than narrative fiction, and would suggest to English teachers generally that they try their hand on using drama with the latter first.

What is the best way to use the book?

There is a progressive structure to the book – basically given by the narrative thread of Mike's 'development'. But I have tried to write it so that the reader can start at any point that is of immediate interest or concern, and move about as need or curiosity dictates. Thus the reader might want to begin with one of the general chapters, or might want to turn first to one of the journal entries which ties in with work s/he is currently attempting. The titles of the general chapters should indicate clearly what they contain and I have given 'headlines' to the journal entries so that the reader can see at a glance the areas they each cover. The headlines are intended both to guide the reader into the journal entry, and also to act as a summary or review that the reader can turn to after reading the journal entry.

2
JOURNAL ONE:
DRAGON SLAYER

Drama as a 'way in' to narrative text

- barriers for children identified and strategies devised to overcome these
- role places children (loosely defined as 'experts') as active interrogators of text
- incompleteness of materials; an invitation to speculation and hypothesizing; active making of meaning from text

Some functions of teacher role

- role as an efficient tool for imparting information and placing children in a clear and specific relationship to a problem, issue or set of materials
- role here used is very similar to a teacher's normal classroom functions – chairing discussions, organizing work tasks – therefore feels 'safe' to a teacher starting to use role
- nevertheless teacher role and children's role as experts give a genuinely different 'feel' to what on the surface look like conventional classroom tasks

- teacher's stance in role as 'one who doesn't know' (equality of status with pupils before a common problem) is important in generating pupil energy and responsibility for learning
- teacher's use of language appropriate to the fictional context is important to create belief in that fictional context and to enable the children to find appropriate language and modes of thinking

Language opportunities

- active comprehension/higher reading skills (interrogating text)
- speculating, hypothesizing
- small group talk: informal, tentative, exploratory
- formal public exposition of hypotheses
- 'getting inside' the style of a narrative

Some aspects of pupil role

- no requirement here to 'act', only to think like archaeologists/historians

Materials and space

- care in reorganizing physical environment to suit learning task and to represent fictional environment
- selection/creation of materials (documents and tweezers) to create significance and authenticity in the drama

Still image (waxworks)

- use to encapsulate results of group thinking/speculating

Tried something new (new for me) recently – some drama. It didn't feel a lot like drama, like what I'd thought of as drama, but Maggie assures me it *was* drama. It worked pretty well, though now I can see ways it might work even better another time.

I'd been casting around for a way of helping 2K to get more out of Rosemary Sutcliff's *Dragon Slayer* than other classes seemed to have done in previous years. There were always a few kids who were enthralled by the book, but many seemed to find the book's style and language a problem. Sutcliff has simplified the narrative line of *Beowulf* and retold it in modern English but keeps something of the original's style – its rhetorical devices, complex sentence structure, and its archaic vocabulary. These seem to be a real problem for many kids of this age, instead of a challenge they rise to, and it turns them off the book. I'm excited by the book every time I read it, and that's a lot of times now. But how to get *them* to share this excitement?

Chatting to Maggie in the staffroom, I mentioned my worries about *Dragon Slayer*. She said what she often does, 'Why don't you try some drama?' Gets a bit monotonous really. She does a lot of drama work with her English classes – but she's got a lot more confidence and experience than I have, and she knows something about drama, which I don't. I made one of my usual evasive replies and turned the conversation another way.

But next day I found a copy of a magazine, *2D*, in my pigeon-hole in the staffroom. It was turned inside out to show a particular page on which there was a large green mark and a scribbled, 'This might suit. Maggie'. The extract she had marked said:

A similar technique was used to introduce *Beowulf* to a mixed ability group. Extracts from the poem were copied in large italic letters, browned in the oven to age them and torn to fragments. Pupils in groups were given a packet of pieces which made up one fragment and were asked to imagine that they were archaeologists who had discovered the ancient document, trying to decide what it was. When eventually the full text was read in the classroom some of the difficulties were dissolved by virtue of the fact that the class were familiar with some of the lines and because they had approached the text with the sense that this was an ancient document and something of a mystery, and were receptive to its content.

Things clicked rapidly into place. I could see how this approach might well arouse the curiosity of 2K and help the 'strangeness' of *Dragon Slayer* become fascinating, instead of alienating. That night I browned six extracts in the oven, tore each into fragments, removed certain key (give away) words, and placed each in an envelope marked 'British Museum'. I'd chosen extracts (all from the early part of the book) which I thought would give the flavour of the narrative and some clues to its overall structure, so that the kids could engage in the business of deducing what sort of past world it had come from, and what the (missing) remainder of the narrative might be like – in other words to do what historians and archaeologists do with their primary source material.

Extracts used

☐ indicates word removed or illegible.

1

HE LEANED FORWARD ON THE GREAT CARVED SEAT. A SMALL MAN WITH HIS HANDS ON HIS KNEES AND HIS LONGSIGHTED SEAMAN'S GAZE COMING AND GOING ABOUT THE SMOKY HALL AND TOLD AMONG LESSER MATTERS HOW HROTHGA☐ THE GREAT WARRIOR KING OF THE ☐ISH FOLK HAD BUILT FOR HIMSELF A MIGHTY MEAD HALL WHERE HE AND HIS HOUSEHOLD WARRIORS MIGHT FEAST.

2

☐ THE MANWOLF THE DEATHSHADOW WHO HAS HIS LAIR AMONG THE SEA INLETS AND THE

COASTA☐MARSHES. HE HEARD THE LAUGHTER AND THE☐HARP SONG FROM☐THE KING'S HIGH HALL AND IT TROUBLED HIM IN HIS DARK DREAMS AND HE ROUSED AND CAME UP OUT OF THE WASTE LANDS AND SNUFFED ABOUT THE PORCH.

3

WHEN MY FATHER NEEDED A FRIEND AT HIS SHOULDER HE FOUND SUCH A ONE IN THIS HROTHGAR OF THE☐BE☐SAID. SHELTER HE GAVE TO MY FATHER AN☐MY FIRST MEMORIES ARE OF LYING ON☐A WOLFSKIN IN FRONT OF HIS FIRE. HE PAID THE☐THE FINE FOR THE MAN MY

4

HROTHGAR'S COAST WARDEN SITTING ON THE CLIFFTOP NORTHWARD FROM HEOROT SAW A STRANGE VESSEL RUNNING IN FROM THE OPEN SEA BETWEEN THE HIGH HEADLANDS AT THE MOUTH OF THE FJORD. A WAR GALLEY LONG AND SLIM AND SWIFT AND THE LIGHT BLINKED IN THE PAINTED SHIELDS HUNG ALONG HER BULWARKS AND THE GREY BATTLEGEAR OF THE MEN WHO SWUNG THE OARS HER STRIPED SAIL FELL SLACK.

5

HE STEPPED ACROSS THE DOOR SILL ON TO THE MANY COLOURED FLAGSTONES OF THE FLOOR. DOWN THE MIDST OF THE HALL THE FIRES BLAZED ON THEIR THREE HEARTHS. AND THE SMOKE CURLED UPWARDS TO FIND ITS WAY OUT☐ THROUGH THE OPENINGS IN THE ROOF HIGH OVERHEAD AND HE SAW THE WARRIORS AT THEIR LONG TABLES WITH BOAR FLESH AND HUGH PILES OF BARLEY CAKES BEFORE THEM. SAW TOO THE ROOF TRE

6

HE CAME TO THE FOREPORCH AND SNUFFLED
ABOUT IT AND SMELLED THE MAN SMELL AND
FOUND THAT THE DOOR WAS BOLTED. SNARLING IN
RAGE THAT ANY DARE KEEP HIM OUT HE SET THE
FLAT OF HIS TALON TIPPED HANDS AGAINST THE
TIMBERS AND BURST THEM IN. DARK AS IT WAS THE
HALL SEEMED TO FILL WITH A MONSTROUS
SHADOW AT HIS COMING. HIS TWO EYES GLOWED
WITH A GHASTLY WAVERING GREEN FLAME.
LAUGHING HE SEIZED

Monday came around and with it the double period when I
planned to start looking at *Dragon Slayer* with the class. But
these 'ancient remnants', not the paperback itself, were to be
their introduction to the story. I'd arranged the classroom as in
Figure 1.
After I'd asked 2K to sort themselves into six groups, and then
sit in the semicircle of chairs, I told them very briefly that

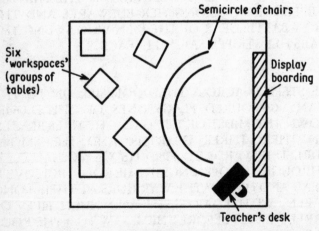

Figure 1

today's work was going to be a little different from usual and then straight away began to speak to them as a museum curator addressing experts in his own field:

Ladies and gentlemen, I'm delighted that you were able to come here to the British Museum at such short notice. Doubtless you are all wondering why you've been asked to come together here from all over the country, especially in such a hurry. The fact is we need your assistance, your expertise, to help us make sense of one of the most important finds to be brought to the Museum for many, many years.

I spoke seriously, almost solemnly – I could see 2K weren't sure what to make of it, but they were intrigued. I'd 'scripted' and 'rehearsed' my words pretty carefully, feeling that what I wanted needed setting up rather exactly and impromptu words might send things off in quite a wrong direction.

I then 'revealed' the find, in the six envelopes, and spoke of 'fragments of an ancient document' which needed piecing together and interpreting.

'We must ask: what do the words say?
            what kind of document are they from?
            how do the six fragments relate to each
              other?
            to what kind of place and time do they
              belong?'

I asked them to begin by assembling their torn fragment, trying to read what it said and to transcribe it. This was to be done in the 'workspaces'. Each group was given an envelope and asked to treat the contents with great care. Then I sent them to the workspaces with these words:

At present we know very little of these fragments. We know they are genuine. We know they are very, very old. They seem to me like a mysterious voice calling from the past, speaking to us across the centuries. Our task is to try to understand that voice, to unravel the mysteries of its message. I wish you luck in your task.

I spoke like this because it seemed important, if my plan were to work, that 2K should look at the documents, not just as a group of kids but as *experts*. The activity had to feel 'special' or 'different', so that they were willing to take on the viewpoint of archaeologists. (I didn't want them to 'act' like archaeologists – however archaeologists might act – but to *think* like archaeologists: use known data to speculate about what wasn't known, and check their speculations against that known data.) Afterwards I thought of ways I could have made the activity feel more 'special' and so help the kids slip more firmly into that archaeologist's viewpoint. For example, I think it would have helped to underline the preciousness of the charred fragments if I had asked them not to touch them with their fingers, but only to handle them with a small pair of tweezers. (Where would I get six small pairs of tweezers? Science department?)

I was pleased by the way the class got down to working at the task. My introduction seemed to have 'grabbed' their interest, though generally the boys were more involved and seemed to have taken on the archaeologist's viewpoint more than the girls. As they worked I went around trying to remain curator and not teacher. Maggie had talked with me on various occasions about teaching 'in role', but it had always seemed a very risky affair to me. Here I felt comfortable – the role of curator meant that I was organizing, supporting, supervising (like a teacher) and yet somehow it had a different 'feel' – I'm not sure how to define it – and I'm sure the task of deciphering, transcribing and interpreting had a different 'feel' for the kids from a lot of teacher-originated tasks.

Here's what happened when one group excitedly asked me to come over and see them:

Teacher: We've had a bit of a breakthrough, have we?
          Gosh, there's quite a bit missing here, isn't there?

Pupil 1: It says something about his father doing something to a man and lying on a wolf-skin . . . or . . .

Pupil 2: Yeah – *him* lying on a wolf-skin

Pupil 1: Lying on a wolf-skin. And theirs over there, it's got something about a man-wolf.

Teacher: So wolf seems to be a sort of . . . er . . .

Pupil 2: Link.

Teacher: A link. . . . Does it help us at all to guess at where or when this document was written? Does the wolf idea give any clues about place or time?

Pupil 2: Scandinavia?

Pupil 3: No, more likely England, because they used to have wolves in England.

Teacher: So you think it's a native English document?

Pupil 2: Yes – because why should they move it all this way?

Pupil 3: And they did have wolves in England.

One moment when I wasn't sure what to do came as I approached another group:

Pupil: Are these real? Or are they just made up?

Teacher: Let's assume they're real, shall we?

Pupil: No but *are* they real?

Teacher: Let's *assume* they're real.

I didn't feel I'd dealt with this satisfactorily, though the group let it drop and continued working at the task. It was interesting that at various times I overheard a number of comments around the room about 'baking paper in the oven to make it look old', but these same kids who obviously recognized that the documents were 'made up' were still treating them as 'real' in their role as 'experts'. I suppose I needed to find a way of telling that particular girl that the documents were, in a different sense, both 'real' and 'made up'. I'm still not sure how I'd manage it though.

One definite mistake I made was to invite the researchers to look at the fragments other groups were examining. I did this too early, so that one or two kids went wandering without ever really having time to get absorbed by their own documents. Another time I'd leave this invitation till much later, and perhaps organize it more tightly to make it a more definite phase in the work, or even not do it at all, because the next stage brought the experts and their fragments all together.

Having called them all back together, I addressed them again as the curator, asking them to offer any comments or questions. It was obvious that quite a number of the kids were searching hard for patterns and explanations – the recurrence of the wolf-motif in the documents came up frequently. Then:

Teacher: Can we try and pull this together a bit? You have all been examining different fragments. What can we do to try and look at it a bit more as a whole?
Pupil: Try to sort out the different pieces. Say it was a book – then you would sort out which pages go where.
Teacher: So we're talking about putting it in order.
Pupil: Yeah.

I was delighted. This suggestion was exactly what I'd hoped for. I put all six collated fragments up on the display board (each group had assembled and mounted theirs on a piece of card with Blutack I'd supplied) accompanied by the transcripts the group had made. The transcripts were all read aloud and discussed briefly. I was trying hard to restrict my comments to 'chairing', to echo points made by the group or occasionally prompt a hesitant speaker. Maggie's words about teacher in role as 'someone who doesn't know, someone who shares the group's puzzlement or predicament' ran through my head, and I *think* I managed to resist the teacherly temptation to seize on and emphasize the 'correct' points, or the observations that I knew would lead somewhere. What was important I felt was the kids' active involvement in teasing out a puzzle, in constructing a hypothesis. They didn't have to be 'right' – they could check their theories out later when they read the book.

Then I got panicked by time (the bell was almost due) and

unfortunately rushed the class into some hasty and not very well considered decisions about the order of the fragments. I knew this was wrong as I was doing it, but once launched I somehow couldn't stop myself and say, 'Perhaps we shouldn't rush this – perhaps we can all think about the problem and come back with our ideas next time we meet'.

Maggie was quite taken aback when I cornered her in the staffroom and gave her a blow-by-blow account of the session. She had the good grace not to say, 'I told you so', but I did notice a little (triumphant?) smile at my excitement. In a few minutes she'd helped me plan out the next session: we'd look at the documents again (in role in the Museum), talk through the order more fully and try to arrive (as a whole group) at a general consensus about the gist of the overall story in the documents, and about the period and place of their writing. Then each group would create a 'waxwork' to put in the Museum, alongside their document and the transcript. The waxwork would be a 'group sculpture' or 'still image' made by the group, using their own bodies. It would demonstrate their hypothesis of what their own extract depicted and/or of the events and circumstances they guessed surrounded it (the extracts chosen from *Dragon Slayer* occurred at shortish intervals in the early part of the book, chosen so that it was possible to make inferences about the gaps). They were to work out a spoken commentary which one of the group would deliver to accompany and explain the waxwork. The sequence of waxworks and commentaries would represent the Museum's display, which explained to the public their hypothesis about the new find.

I didn't do it. The rest of my time that week with 2K was a double period and a single. I lost the double because they were on a visit, and I felt the single period was too short, and I ought to get some writing out of them this week, so we worked on a short piece they were to complete at home. By the time next Monday came round all sorts of doubts and anxieties had appeared. Did I really understand this group sculpture business and could I get it to work? Could I afford the time? Christmas was looming and we were going to be short of time just to read the book. And so on and so on. So I 'chickened out'. It's a pity. When I gave out the books that Monday and explained that the documents were in fact extracts from *Dragon Slayer*, the kids were very eager to get into the novel, and they did throughout take the style of the book more in their stride than previous groups had done. But I'm sure that if I'd gone on as planned they'd have coped even better – they would have had time to construct a considered hypothesis about the narrative, and about the time and place of derivation. That theory could have been recorded. (Polaroid instant photos of the waxworks and writing down of the spoken commentaries.) We might even have had a go at writing our own version of the gaps in the narrative, so that the kids could really get 'inside' the style. Then our reading of *Dragon Slayer* would have been informed by the key themes or motifs which our original enquiry had raised – so that the book had a *pattern* from the outset – and by the questions the kids wanted answered and the hypotheses they were keen to check.

Well, there's always next year.

It's only just occurred to me that the ancient documents I'd prepared were a marvellous comprehension exercise: one that was quite demanding yet one they'd coped with incredibly well – many of their inferences were spot on! Perhaps they coped so well because it didn't feel like a comprehension exercise. And perhaps I've blundered on a way I can work on 'higher reading skills' without resorting to those sterile exercises from text-books quite so often?

3
SOME ASSUMPTIONS

English is about working on the knowledge we have acquired from the unsystematic processes of living, about giving expression to it and making it into a firmer and more conscious kind of living.

Peter Medway (1980, p. 8)

Drama enables children to understand what they know, but do not yet know they know.

Dorothy Heathcote (to students at Newcastle University)

English and drama ought not to be such awkward bedfellows. I see them as an ideal couple – they have a huge amount in common, yet at the same time their own distinctive individual characters. Theirs *ought* to be a satisfying and fruitful relationship: each able to be their own person, but both able to find support and enrichment from the other in their common values and complementary activities. But somehow this sense of partnership is often missing and neither one seems able to offer to, or take from, the other what they might. Both seem to retreat constantly into the shells of their individual identities and to engage in a process of self-affirmation which prevents either from seeing the real potentialities of the other.

I want to challenge the essentially *limited* vision that English and drama teachers have of each other's practice. The common ground they share is enormous. Often practitioners and theorists in either area will talk about their own values in terms that (did they but realize it!) are interchangeable. If I were to swap the words 'English' and 'drama' in the quotations with which I began, I could take Medway's words into a gathering of drama teachers and Heathcote's to a group of English specialists, and have each nodding sagely at the importance of their own discipline for the education of young people, without any recognition of the common ground. I could dwell a long time on defining that common ground here, but since all that follows is devoted to an exploration of this territory, I will only say this:

> *Both can (as Heathcote and Medway indicate) bring into consciousness our implicit, intuitive and affective understandings, so that we can examine them, employ them, and link them with our intellectual understandings in a holistic way of knowing ourselves and the world.*
>
> *Both mediate these understandings through fictional forms, in which language occupies a central place.*

I think it important that I sketch out here my assumptions about the teaching of English, and drama's place within it:

1   For me the most comfortable, versatile and powerful way of working in the English classroom is one where the reading of fiction, language work and drama activities are closely related; indeed grow out of, and feed, each other (see Figure 2).

How this can happen is amplified later so I will not dwell on it here.

2   I place a high priority in English work and in drama upon creating opportunities for shared experiences in the classroom.

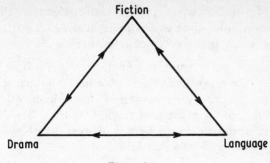

Figure 2

I believe with David Hargreaves that a high priority for schools is the creation of 'solidary experiences' (1982). It used to be said that 'drama is concerned with the individuality or individuals, with the uniqueness of each human essence' (Way, 1967, 3). *It is not.* Yes of course we must recognize the individuality of children, but the medium of drama is one in which ideas are explored and shaped *in groups*; where the contribution of each individual affects, and is modified by, those or others; where experience and reflection are shared and public.

Because of the priority I accord to creating opportunities for shared/solidary experience, I place great value on the use of a shared class reader (*as well as* individual reading and language work) and I tend to use a whole group framework in drama (though much individual and small group work may be done within that overall framework).

3   Many English teachers will encounter certain key problems in using drama, due to the habits of mind acquired in English teaching.

a) They think or assume that drama operates like story. It doesn't. See Chapter 7, where I discuss the differences.

b) They will tend to keep pulling away from the drama encounter into discussion; away from a first person to a third person viewpoint; from moment-to-moment experience in 'now' time to discursive analysis. A particularly clear example of this comes in Journal 4.

Although I am assuming that English teachers will use drama for their own purposes as English teachers (and that will give their drama work a different emphasis to the drama specialist), they still need to respect and employ the basic 'laws' of the medium of drama if they wish it to work for them. I shall attempt to summarize some of these laws here:

1 Drama explores human actions, attitudes, values and relationships, through a shared fiction, by means of an agreement to pretend.
2 This fiction operates in the present tense, in 'now' time: participants engage with the events of the drama as they are happening.
3 The 'now' of drama is heavy with a sense of the impending, of the future, of the consequences of present actions: the interaction between present and future, action and consequence, creates tension, which is the driving force of drama.
4 Sequencing in drama is built of a succession of 'present moments', a series of episodes. The sequence these occur in may coincide outwardly with a natural, narrative sequence (though the inner structuring of the 'moments' will not be narrative structuring), or it may be one that moves backward and forward in time, or one that examines a situation through a succession of differing viewpoints.
5 In drama we examine actions, attitudes, values and relationships from a dual viewpoint: from the viewpoint of those involved – we 'become' or 'represent' the people in the drama – and also from our own viewpoint – as people making, and reflecting on, the drama. So we examine them both 'hot' and 'cold': as participant and as spectator.
6 In drama (as in dance) the primary medium of expression is the person: expression in the main is not mediated through other materials, as in the visual and literary arts, or as often

happens in music. Drama statements are made primarily through the movement and stillness, the sounds and silence of the participants – or to put it another way they employ the same ordinary resources of signalling and communication as they use in their everyday actions and interactions.

4
JOURNAL TWO: 'THE WAY WEST'

Working from a theme – 'Wagon Train'

- need to identify aims and learning areas within the theme
- finding a specific focus within the theme (according to your aims)
- selection of materials, according to focus required. Materials need to have an 'unfinished' quality about them – to provoke response from pupils.

How to plan and yet be open to children's ideas

- requires clarity about aims
- requires clarity about which decisions teacher must reserve and which to give to the class

Building belief and seriousness in drama

- need to make explicit what teacher is expecting from children in a drama – not 'acting' but adopting a viewpoint
- dealing with flippant contributions

I've been trying various bits of drama with 1S. Since the *Dragon Slayer* work, I've wanted to experiment a bit more with drama activities, and I felt safest doing this with my first year. I've done several sessions now and keep running into certain problems.

I seem to assume too much and make leaps which leave the children behind, so they don't always understand the task I am giving them. I need to learn to break down tasks into clearer, more manageable stages, and to explain them clearly.

I don't find it easy to get the children to go beyond a fairly superficial 'play' level of doing drama. They regard it as 'fun', as a relief from other more formal activities – which in a sense is fair enough, but it means that they don't really 'engage' with the material. I'd like the drama to be fun but demanding fun, if that makes sense.

Although I know it's important to try and use children's ideas to build the drama, I often feel insecure in teaching drama and tend to ignore or deflect their ideas so that they fit my predetermined plan.

So in this lesson with 1S, my aims were to:

1 Make sure that the children clearly understood the nature of the task and manner of working required of them: that meant breaking down the task into manageable elements or units.
2 Use appropriate strategies to help build seriousness and belief in the drama.
3 Create an atmosphere where the children felt confident to contribute their ideas, and endeavour as teacher to make use of their ideas.

I found a 'structure' as they term it, in *Drama Structures* by O'Neill and Lambert (1982), which seemed to me to offer scope for these three aims. It's called 'The Way West'; I decided to adapt this. Basically my plan was in three parts.

1 Establishing information and context through the use of visual stimulus materials, teacher talk and class discussion.

2 Pair work to establish individual identities and individual reasons for going West.
3 Whole group meeting – interested people come to find out more about the journey and the offer of free land in Oregon.

Phase one: building the context

THE PHOTOGRAPH

I began by showing the class a photograph of a group of settlers and their wagons from *Drama Structures*.

The photo aroused their interest and pulled them together physically as a group in order to see it.

I asked them a series of questions about the photograph:
What does the photo suggest to you?
How long ago do you think it was taken?
What sort of people do you think they are?
What sort of feelings or mood come across to you?
I then told them the 'facts' about the photo: that these were poor settlers travelling to seek a new life in the American West in the last century.

I realized before I had gone very far that I had set about things in the wrong order. I had planned a drama about 'The Way West', and so I had no right to be asking questions that sounded open (though they weren't) about who the people in the photograph were.
When a boy said they looked like gypsies, I knew I had a choice: to abandon my plan, or ignore/divert his suggestion. I was wedded to my plan and so I took the second option.

In retrospect I can see that I had available to me two ways of using the photo.

i) To begin by explaining who the people were, then invite comment on their mood and feeling, as a way of moving the class into the drama.

ii) To begin with genuinely open questioning about who the people might be and what the photograph told us of their life and circumstances. This would only be legitimate if I were not committed to 'The Way West', but prepared to work on gypsies, refugees or whatever else came up.

FACTS, POSTERS, MAPS

I told the children some facts about the Oregon Trail – the period, location, the offer of free land, the length of the journey.

I showed them a very basic map of the Oregon Trail which I had drawn on sugar paper. It showed the mountain ranges, the rivers and deserts to be crossed and the fertile land which was their destination. We talked about the map. I tried to give some idea of scale by showing how England could be put down and lost in that vast continent. I asked, 'How long do you think it would take them to cover 2000 miles of difficult country in their wagons?' I pointed out to the children several

Basically in this part of the lesson I lost my way, tried to feed in far too much information, without really being clear about where I was heading, and lost the initial interest of many of the children. This discussion went on far too long (25 minutes) and by the end of it, I was spending quite a lot of time picking up 'errant behaviour' and trying to hold the attention of the class.

I think the visual material (map and posters) was sound, but just got lost in the general morass of detail. My attempts to get the children to understand the scale of the journey (both in distance and time) didn't succeed at all. I invited them to think of their posters I had made on sugar paper and displayed on the walls of the hall, where we were working. These advertised the offer of free land in Oregon and invited those interested to attend a meeting.

We discussed some of the reasons why people might have decided to make the difficult and dangerous journey.

In order to bring home the difficulty and danger, I produced another piece of sugar paper on which I had drawn a cross with the inscription:

> Mary Ellis
> Died May 7th 1845
> Age 2 months

(O'Neill and Lambert, 1982, 34)

I told them that a wooden cross with this inscription had been found years later by the side of the Oregon Trail.

own experiences of travelling and translate these. For example a car or coach from Leicester to London along the M1: how long would it take on foot along rough tracks? This didn't really help them.

How do you convey the idea of such vast distances and such slow progress with any felt immediacy?

I'm not sure I can grasp it myself.

The cross produced a marked change in the class. They rapidly became attentive and absorbed, particularly when a boy commented that the child had probably been born on the journey.

I think I should have been much more selective and economical with stimulus material and information. Thinking about it afterwards, it occurred to me that I might have been much better off starting straight in from the posters:

i) Ask the children to look at the posters, then discuss their meaning and questions arising.

ii) Ask what kinds of people might be interested in going on such a journey.

iii) Move into the advertised meeting.

I had a real opportunity, which I didn't take, when the class grew so interested in the death of Mary Ellis. I realize now that I should have shifted my ground, and concentrated on the baby, abandoning my original plan. In fact, I felt this at the time, but wasn't sure how to do it. It seemed a big jump from my plan, which sought to build up slowly an investment in deciding to go on the journey, and looking at the baby's death would have meant leaping ahead to the middle of the journey. I suppose there's no reason not to make that leap, but I couldn't see a way. And I felt that they needed to know more about their own identities and reasons for going on, before coping with the difficulties of the journey. At any rate, I pressed on with my plan.

The plan was to do a series of activities which I hoped would help the children to create an identity for themselves, now that the overall context of the drama had been established. Here I was particularly keen not to make leaps or assumptions and leave the children puzzled or confused, so I had a sequence which I hoped would allow them to consolidate their identity within the drama steadily:

Phase two: building an identity

WRITTEN TASK

I asked them to close their eyes and imagine they were one of the people in the photograph I had shown earlier. I asked:

This seems to me to be a useful strategy at times – isolating the children and asking them to write down some information about their

What sort of person are you?

Why did you choose to make the journey?
I then gave them paper and asked each to write their reasons for going.

role helps ensure that all have made a few decisions because they have to commit them to paper.
I was disappointed in what they wrote. They were just giving me back what I had given them earlier, but then I hadn't done anything to extend their thinking about motives for going.

PAIR WORK

'A has heard about the wagon train setting off to Oregon and is keen to join it. A tells B his/her reasons.'
Then I asked the children to reverse roles and repeat the exercise.

They tackled this willingly, though fairly lightheartedly – relieved I suppose to be *doing* something. I don't think it helped them move towards belief in their role. It was a fairly contextless exercise – why was A telling B? what was B's attitude? who *was* B? – with no very clear purpose.

REPORTING BACK

I gathered the class and we listened to the reasons they had chosen.

Again the same reasons came back – my attempt at consolidation had turned out to be not much more than repetition. The children didn't listen well – I think because they felt they were re-treading old ground.

In my concern to not make leaps which lost the children and to build steadily, I had broken down the process of selecting a motivation too far, into too many steps. Yes, each activity was clear and the children knew what was expected of them at each stage, but the overall direction and purpose was no longer clear. Another point is that I asked them to think as individuals about why they were interested in going, whereas in fact it would have been mainly groups (families, friends, business partners) who travelled on the Oregon Trail, and it would have been more appropriate for the children to sort out their reasons for going in a group context, for example in a family discussion.

The next stage in my plan was to hold a meeting with the children in role as people interested in the offer of free land in Oregon and myself in role as a 'Government Land Agent' there to explain the scheme and answer questions.

Phase three: the meeting

I asked a group to arrange some chairs as they thought appropriate for such a meeting.

A mistake! I ended up with just two long sprawling rows of chairs, which made focusing the attention of the class in the meeting difficult. *Lesson*: think carefully about the physical layout and use of space necessary to an activity and if it needs to be a certain way, get it that way. Don't give choices that can mess up essential conditions for an activity!

The meeting began. As Government Land Agent I made a brief speech about the offer of free land, then

The children had no difficulty in accepting me in a role as Government Land Agent. The role wasn't all invited queries. I said I believed some people present had first-hand knowledge of Oregon and the trail, and that they as well as I could tell the rest about what would lie in store for the settlers.

that far removed from being teacher. I offered the opportunity for some to 'know about' Oregon, hoping that in this way the building of a sense of anticipation about the journey could be shared – they could take some responsibility for it.

One boy in particular, Robin, seized the 'power opportunity' this offered and told a series of horrific tales about murders committed by the Indians, in a very exaggerated 'American' accent. He was playing to the gallery, and succeeding, getting a lot of laughs. He had displayed this kind of behaviour quite often before. I tried, not very successfully, to fend this off, suggesting that such stories did get around but were often exaggerated and asked if others could give a more balanced view. But time ran out on me – the meeting had begun ten minutes before the bell – and we ended with the class in frivolous mood, after seventy minutes of trying to get seriousness and belief!

I was dismayed when Robin took control and systematically destroyed what I had been working for. I felt helpless. I'd issued the invitation; he'd responded to it. I felt that I couldn't just stop the drama and rebuke him or tell him that what he was doing was inappropriate. The situation was my fault, not his, and I felt trapped – quite at a loss what to do, except to struggle on in role, trying to get other children to come to my rescue.

A final thought about the meeting. The way in which I set it up was bogus. It was a meeting to decide *whether* to go, although for the drama to continue (as I intended it should) they would *all* have to decide to go. As it happened time ran out before I could ask them to decide so I was saved the problem of finding that half of them had thought better of it.

Maggie's response to my notes

What an interesting collection of problems this lesson threw up!

I think you are on to one of the root problems when you write about being more selective. What a wealth of good materials you had ready for this lesson, but they were largely wasted because there were far, far too many of them. *But* if you are to be selective you need to know what it is you want from a lesson. You had some admirable aims for yourself *as teacher*, but what about *aims for the children's learning*?

Yes, they were to do a drama about a wagon train, but that doesn't tell you much. You need to think about what human experiences, choices and dilemmas are offered in being on a wagon train – then about which seem appropriate to the class, which they can cope with, and which might offer useful learning areas. In other words: *What is your focus?* A drama about a wagon train journey might be about:

risking everything on a gamble, and having to trust what others tell us;
getting used to new neighbours / making new friends;
deciding what to leave behind;
wondering if we can trust the wagon-master on whom all our lives depend;
weighing the opportunities the journey offers to the younger members of the family, against the risk to the older ones (will Granny survive the journey?);

learning to cope with physical privation and constant discouragement;

tackling tasks for which you have no training – e.g. caring for oxen, repairing a wagon wheel, building your own house;

Remember drama can only be about *one thing at a time*. As it develops, that thing (your focus) will change, but you can only have one focus at any one time. I think part of your problem was that you didn't know what you wanted 'The Way West' to be about. Once you know what you want, you can:

a) select appropriate materials and strategies;
b) make it clear to the children what the direction and purpose of the work is. If you don't know, how can they?

Suppose we look at different ways you could have used your materials in a more selective way to achieve a specific focus:

1 *Focus*: Weighing the pros and cons of the journey.
   Initial stimulus: Your poster.
   Followed by
   Very brief explanation: Facts about the Oregon Trail.
   Discussion: What kinds of people in what kinds of circumstances might wish to go?
   Small group work: Families. Establish individual identities, then: one has seen the poster, comes home to tell the rest and persuade them to go to the meeting. What are their reactions, questions, etc.?
   The meeting: Roughly as you set it up – teacher in role as Government Land Agent. The map could be used to help your explanation.
   (NB: the assumption is that you tell the class early on that it is about *how* some people decided to go, not *whether* they decided to go – so you're not asking for a bogus decision.)

2 *Focus*: Walking (literally walking) across a continent.
   Initial stimulus: Your map with

Brief explanation of free land offer, then

Your photo: Ignore everything else and get the children to look at the people's feet: most are barefooted. And how long would the man's boots have lasted on a trek like that? Explain that the wagons carried possessions and one or two people. The rest would have to walk.

Individual/pair work: After six weeks and 700 miles (a third of the way – the easiest third), tending the blisters on your feet or trying to repair a pair of boots (your only pair) which are beyond repair, and wondering how your feet will cope with the 1300 miles still to go.

(NB: *you don't always have to begin at the beginning in drama*. In fact, with something like 'The Way West' it may be better to start in the middle, and if you choose a focus like tending sore feet, you don't need a lot of information before you move into the drama.)

3 *Focus*: Death of a baby on the wagon train.

Initial stimulus: After two sentences of explanation about the Oregon land-rush in the 1840s, show your cross with Mary Ellis's funeral inscription.

Discussion: Class are asked what questions occur to them to ask about the epitaph and the baby, etc., and to speculate about the answers to their own questions. Get the children to think about the implications of the possible answers.

Whole class still image: of the baby's funeral, built up by stages. First a group is chosen or volunteers to be the baby's family. Then the rest of the class place the family around the grave as they feel is appropriate. (It's probably easier for the volunteers if they are 'placed', rather than having to place themselves.) Then the class place themselves in relation to the family according to how they feel: e.g. sympathetic, or anxious because of delays and impatient to get on with the journey. The whole image is then frozen, and held. Then, perhaps,

Soliloquy: Each person / some people are asked to speak out

loud in role (soliloquize) the thoughts or feelings they
have at that moment.

(NB: the setting up of the still image will probably be a slow
business because you are asking the children to create a
wealth of implications about feelings and relationships
through the still positions. A lot of discussion and trying of
alternative positions for the bereaved family will probably
be necessary.)

Each of these three starts has a different focus, and will give a
quite different experience. The first moves into 'The Way West'
through weighing and discussing the pros and cons. Probably
good for a class who find it easy to work into drama through
talk. The second quickly gives controlled physical activity, and
employs a highly concrete sign (sore feet!). The third moves
straight into an area of strong feeling, though in a manner that
offers considerable 'protection'. You have to choose between
them or any others on the basis of what you want the children
to experience and learn, and what you feel they can cope
with. The third would move too rapidly into emotion and
relationships for some classes.

Another key question you are worrying at in your notes on this
lesson is: *How can teachers create flexible plans?* That is, plans
that accommodate both teacher's aims and the need for children to have a significant hand in shaping the drama. A key to
this, I think, is being absolutely clear about what decisions you
as teacher want or need to reserve to yourself, and which you
are happy for or want the children to make. In your lesson the
children were not free to decide the context, nor were they free
within the drama to decide whether they would or would not
go on the Oregon Trail. These were teacher decisions. The
limited areas of choice they did have at this stage were about
their identity and the particular reasons they had for going
West. Also you allowed them to create the physical layout
for the meeting, which in the event you felt was a mistake. It
might help you in your planning to write the plan in two

columns: *Things I shall decide* and *Things the children will decide*

Any lesson will be a mixture of teacher-decisions and child-decisions – the balance will be determined by particular purposes and circumstances. Remember that decisions are of very different kinds. They can be about:

Context: Who shall we say these people in the photograph are?

Theme/focus: Is this play going to be about learning to trust a new group of people, or about being tricked and betrayed by false promises?

Grouping: Would it be better to tackle this in small groups? And how should the groups be chosen?

Form: How should we place Mary Ellis's family around the grave?

Procedures: What's the best way to conduct this discussion?

Plot: What should happen next?

Role allocation: Who will be the wagon-master?

and so on.

It's important to be clear about what *kinds* of decision you are asking the children to make, and which at all costs you must hold on to! If you'd been clearer about that then you would have known what to do when the children suddenly got interested in Mary Ellis's funeral inscription. If switching to the baby's death doesn't lose you the learning areas you are after, and the decisions that you know you have to keep to yourself, then the switch is no problem. If it does lose these, you cannot make the switch, unless you decide on the spot to go for a new learning area! Many teachers are not clear about this. They just have a gut feeling that it is 'a good thing' for the children to make decisions and have a significant hand in shaping the work. But because it's as vague as that they either offer total choice, which the children won't cope with, or, as you did, operate structures where all the real decisions were the teacher's, and the children really have very little hand in the work – though the style of operating and questioning suggests that they are being given the chance to make choices.

FINALLY, SOME THOUGHTS ABOUT ROBIN

Essentially I think you needed to stop the drama to look with the class at what was happening. (Having said this I'm not sure how well this would have worked *at that moment* – a few minutes from the end of the lesson, with the class, as you describe it, in frivolous mood. Maybe it could be dealt with more easily when you next meet them, at the beginning of the lesson.)

Robin's behaviour seems to have been a problem because:

(*A*) he threatened your plan;
(*B*) he was undermining the seriousness of the rest of the class.

(*A*) would not really have been a problem if you hadn't, as you say, set up the meeting in a bogus manner – as if it were deciding *whether* to go. For the drama to continue you had to have a unanimous 'yes' – no wonder you panicked when Robin began to put people off going. If the drama had been clearly about 'how we decided to go' *or* genuinely about 'whether to go' it would have been easier to handle, as (*B*) then becomes the sole issue. As I've said, I think what Robin was doing needed examining by you and the class together. I'd like to separate out two aspects of his behaviour: the accent; the content of his contributions.

I'd have had no hesitation in telling him *not* to use the 'American' accent on the grounds that we didn't need it, and that it was making it difficult for others to be serious about the work. (I always try to make it very clear that when I rule something 'out of court' this is because it is undermining the work of the class, not because it is undermining me.)

The content, on the other hand, was fair enough if it was offered seriously, and if you could sort out with Robin and the class its part in the overall dynamic of the drama. In other words, if a man at such a meeting says such things, he must have a reason or a motive: maybe he has interests, or is acting for interests, which would be harmed by a flood of settlers going West; maybe he thinks the Government Land Agent is irresponsible in encouraging people to trek into the wilderness without a real awareness of the dangers; or maybe he is just the local mischief-maker or gossip. I think the best course of action would be to expect Robin and/or the class to define the role motivation and hence the nature of the 'challenge' his role is offering. Then his challenge needn't be a threat to the work, but actually provides the tension which gives that meeting its dynamic:

> Who will win the ear of the audience? How will those interested in the journey judge between the two advocates, or get at their real motivation in order to make a decision with momentous consequences?

Who 'wins' is irrelevant. The drama is the meeting itself, rather than what follows the meeting. (If the meeting is about 'how we decided to go' the class can decide whether such a challenge is something they need in the drama, and if so why they all discount it. It might well be that, if the work had been clearly about 'how we decided to go', the challenge might never have arisen.)

Once the motivation and nature of the challenge have been sorted out through discussion, the drama can be re-played, with the clearly defined tension that challenge brings. What this does is to allow Robin to stay in the centre of the picture, where he obviously wants to be at the moment, but to load that special status with responsibility. It might well be necessary to say publicly to Robin before the meeting is replayed, 'So you will try to persuade all these people not to go. That's a hard job – one you'll have to think a lot about, and think fast. Really, how our drama turns out is going to depend quite a lot on you. Do you think you can manage it?' Maybe Robin will say he can't manage it, and someone else will offer. Maybe he could manage it with support from one or two others. Whoever tackles it, what you have done is make clear your expectations about the way they are going to work in drama, and to signal that a flippant contribution or challenge may be taken on and imbued with significance and seriousness, so that its originator may find himself or herself perforce taking on more than s/he bargained for.

One very final comment about Robin's behaviour. *Could it be that he was behaving in this exhibitionist manner because he was not clear about what drama of the kind you are doing entails? Because he thinks of it as 'acting'?* Do you need to find ways of indicating more clearly to the children that drama is about 'adopting a viewpoint' and not 'acting a character'? In work like that you did on the *Dragon Slayer* material, 'acting' is unlikely to arise. In a drama about wagon trains, it's not surprising if children unused to your way of working think they need to 'act'. So you'll need to help them by explanation, by the way you function in role (i.e. by offering an appropriate model), by setting up role-tasks in ways unlikely to induce 'acting', and when 'acting' does crop up, stopping the work to discuss the problem.

Remember it takes time for anyone to absorb a new way of working – help them all you can.

5
HOW IS A DRAMA
LESSON PLANNED
AND CARRIED OUT?

What follows is an attempt to provide clear guidelines to help the English teacher, unsure of how to proceed, to move into drama. I begin by offering a model of the drama lesson which is clear, simple and flexible (see Figure 3). It is a modified version of a model devised by Brian Watkins (1981, 73).

A number of points need to be made about this model. The boundaries are hazy rather than clear: Enquiry often moves imperceptibly into Definition; likewise Definition into Drama; and there are many ways of promoting Reflection within the Drama as well as after it.

Often the progression in the lesson will not be straight through stages 1 to 4. For example, the teacher may have decided upon the problem to be explored in advance (i.e. the Enquiry stage proper is completed in the teacher's planning), so s/he may begin at stage 2, providing a drama context and theme, or at stage 3, say by immediately adopting a role which both defines the context and theme *and* initiates the drama. Or it may be that the lesson begins with an Enquiry session but proceeds no further than the Definition stage – the problem has

---

1 *Enquiry*
What might the drama be about? Ideas are generated about the context and theme of the drama. Stimulus material, introductory exercises and discussion may all play a part in this process.

---

2 *Definition*
What is the drama about? The teacher provides, or helps the class to find, a context – a particular setting in time, place and action – which allows the drama to begin. The theme or predicament of the drama is established and clarified.

---

3 *Drama*
The class commit themselves to drama, exploring the predicament within the fiction they have established.

---

4 *Reflection*
The class look back on what happened within the drama and explore its consequences and implications.

Figure 3

not been clarified sufficiently for the Drama to begin. This may happen next lesson or the idea may prove to be a blind alley. Or, as usually happens, the class may move frequently out of the Drama for further Definition and/or Reflection, then back again into the Drama. Many drama lessons are characterized by frequent oscillation between these stages. There is no one correct sequence and the model is not intended as a guide in that respect. Its purpose is simply to help teachers to be clear at all times about what stage the work has reached.

It would perhaps be a useful exercise for readers to apply the model to the examples of teaching given in the Journals, to help 'flesh out' the model and make sense of it.

Enquiry and Definition

Although these two stages can merge into one another, what is going on in each is very different.

ENQUIRY IS A 'SCATTERING' PROCESS: GENERATING IDEAS

In response to the teacher's initial stimulus or invitation, the class offer ideas. It is likely that a plethora of possibilities will be raised (see Figure 4).

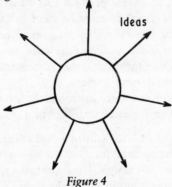

Ideas

Figure 4

DEFINITION IS A NARROWING DOWN PROCESS: SELECTING IDEAS

The teacher assists the class to select a topic or an aspect of a pre-determined topic; then to move from the generalities of the topic to a specific setting in time, place and action (see Figure 5).

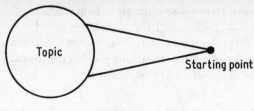

Figure 5

Essentially what is going on in these early stages of the drama lesson is the establishment of:

1 *A contract*. Drama is a collaborative social process which operates through negotiation. Agreement needs to be reached in order that everyone understands the nature of the activity they are about to engage in, its rules and boundaries, and its central core – the predicament the drama is examining. In short, everybody must be clear 'what game we are playing'. In the process of reaching an agreement the class begins to become committed to the work. Because they have a hand in shaping the drama, they are more likely to invest their energies in its development.

2 *A context*. Drama cannot function at the level of generalities – it requires a very specific setting in time, place and action.

The establishment of both contract and context are particularly crucial in the opening stages of the lesson but they are not exclusive to these early stages. The process is a progressive one: there will be re-negotiation and redefinition of contract and context throughout the lesson. Sometimes one can move into drama quickly with a minimal consensus and a fairly low level of commitment, and perhaps a very incomplete definition of context – say with a class who get bored easily if you don't start fast. Here is an example of a lesson opening where contract and context are outlined only minimally before the drama commences:

The teacher sits so that he can make eye-to-eye contact with each member of the class, who are sitting in a bunch or a circle in front of him.

Today we're going to do some drama work . . . but before we start we need to sort out a couple of things. If the drama is to work we shall all need to believe that we are different people – just for now. . . . Do you think we could try that?
Pause. He waits for a response. If 'no'. . . .
No? (*friendly*) Why not?

Discussion of reasons. It is likely to be one or a few who say 'no'. It may be genuine uncertainty or it may be a 'try-on'. Either way the teacher, by pursuing the question 'why not?' indicates that the problem is one which merits attention, and that he takes it seriously because it affects everybody's work. Group pressure, real or implied, can help.

Well, everyone else seems to think they can believe. So that we can all get on and do some drama, are you willing to try? I know it can be hard, but if you give it a go, it'll probably come.
Pause. Teacher nods encouragingly.
OK? Now one more thing, before we start. I'm going to be in the drama too. I can believe that you're someone different. Can you believe that I'm someone else in the drama?
Pause. Teacher looks around smiling.
Right? Great! Now I shall start the drama by being someone else. I'll go over there and when I come back I'll be someone else and the drama will have begun. You'll have to think fast, mind you. There won't be time for explanations. You'll have to pick up clues quickly and act on them. . . . Are you good at picking up clues from what people do and say?
Pause. He looks round enquiringly, supportively.
Right, now the person I'm going to be will come in very fast and expect you to do something very fast. Ready?
(*The teacher has gained a further, though minimal, commitment and has represented the coming task as an intriguing*

challenge to put the class 'on their mettle'. Throughout, the impending drama has been represented as something they will 'make' through their own willingness to try to 'believe'.)

The teacher now goes into role, bursting through an imagined door and barking out:
Right! On your feet! . . . Get a move on, the camp commandant is on his way now! . . . Stand by your beds . . . (*saluting rigidly towards the door*). Attention!

The teacher then stops the play and depending on
  a) How the children have responded,
  b Why he thinks they have so responded,
  c) which pupil or pupils he is addressing,
he might say (sternly):
I thought you said you could believe in it? Do you realize that by behaving like that you are making it difficult for everybody else?
or (smiling warmly):
Did you find it difficult? (*He nods acceptingly to their replies.*) Well, I said it's not always easy. Could we have another go? Perhaps it will be easier when you know what I'm going to do and it's not all such a surprise. That sometimes makes things easier.
or (beaming):
I think we managed to believe in it, don't you?

The teacher then questions the class about what clues they picked up. His role-play has created the beginnings of a drama context rapidly and economically:
Likely setting: hut (with beds) in prison or army camp.
Likely roles for class: prisoners or soldiers.
Attitudes: urgency, expectancy, tension.
By eliciting the children's responses he helps them to define the situation a little more. Discussion of their feelings on being told of the commandant's imminent visit and of the possible reasons for the visit leads into a 're-run'.

(Much of the drama context may remain undefined as yet – e.g. period, individual identities of the children in the drama, why they are in the camp, etc. but there is enough known for their present purposes, and the teacher is using the element of uncertainty as a means of inducing dramatic tension and helping the class to commit themselves to the drama and to work at belief.)

Right. Are we ready to try that bit again? Let's see if we can all believe in it this time. Then perhaps we can find out why on earth the commandant is coming to see you on such a surprise visit.

CONTRACT

Contract is a two-way affair.[1] It involves obligations and responsibilities on both sides – teacher and pupils. At times it may appear one-sided, as for example in this sample opening, where the teacher is laying down very clearly some elements of the way they will be working and some parameters of behaviour. The teacher *has* to do this – has to make it clear to the children what demands working in drama makes on them. But in return the teacher will, through the discussion after the brief initial role-play, indicate that s/he is listening carefully to their ideas and that the fabric of the drama will be woven from their suggestions. The play is built collaboratively: some decisions are made by the class, some by the teacher.

It is important that teachers are very clear in their own minds, and in what they say to the children, about which decisions they are giving to the class to take and which they are making themselves. A very crude classification of types of drama lessons according to this 'decisions-criterion' is:

1 Pupil-initiated and open-ended.
2 Teacher-initiated and open-ended.
3 Teacher-initiated and subsequently teacher-structured to explore a particular teacher-chosen problem, theme, or learning area.

All three are legitimate and most teachers will use all three kinds of lessons at different times. The problem arises when the categories get muddled – say the teacher intends to operate in mode 3 but signals to the class that they are in mode 2 by (a familiar enough trap!) asking open questions and hoping that they will come up with the answers s/he wants (see Journal 2). If the teacher wants to begin the drama in a specific way or to centre it on a particular theme or dilemma s/he must make that clear to the class and not pretend or imagine that the lesson is 'totally open' when in fact it is not and in terms of his teaching intentions cannot be. The teacher who, working on the Battle of Hastings, asks his class, 'How are we going to stop the Normans from overrunning our defences on the hills?' receives the various suggestions they offer unenthusiastically and then, after a pregnant pause, demands, 'Who's going to help me build a stockade?', is unlikely to win a committed response from his class. After apparently being invited to help shape the work, they have discovered that it is, after all, strictly teacher's play.

If the work is in mode 3 – teacher-initiated, with an overall structure planned in advance by the teacher – the children still can, and it is important that they should, contribute significantly to the work. Let us say that the teacher wishes to explore the theme of coping with bullying, by peers and by those in authority. This could easily be explored in a drama context based on Joan Aiken's *Midnight is a Place* (factory setting).[2] The teacher has decided on the setting and the theme but there is still much for the children to contribute and decide: establishing the working and social patterns of the factory; the incidence and direction of the bullying; the responses of the workers within the options open to them in this particular fictional setting; and the moral judgements the children draw from exploring the issue in drama and reflecting on its implications for their own lives.

If the work is in mode 1 – pupil-initiated and open-ended – the teacher is still responsible for helping to structure the work:

finding a form in which the children's ideas can be made to work; helping them to clarify the core of the work; and pointing out implications of the decisions they are considering. (See Journal 2 for a more detailed look at decisions in the drama lesson.)

I have already argued that greater commitment to the drama is likely where children have a significant part in shaping the work. To enable children to become active shapers of the drama, in order to help them understand that they are indeed truly responsible for the work in hand, it is important that the teacher functions as a non-expert, as 'one who does not know'. Too often teachers operate saddled with the burden of their own expertise. They ask questions to which they know the answers, and to which therefore logically there is no need for the pupils to reply. Indeed, there is risk in replying: better to wait in the knowledge that sooner or later the teacher will supply the answer if the class does not. Or if answers are offered, they are not the product of any real thinking, only of a desire to please or placate the teacher.

In drama work the teacher is not the expert in that he knows the right answers. There are no right answers to questions such as: 'What drove this person/these people to commit the murder?'; 'Which would be the most interesting situation to explore?'; 'Can we trust this wagon-master? And if not, here in the wilderness, at the half-way point in our journey, what can we do about it?'; 'How can we find a way of clearly showing the king what it would mean if he destroyed our houses, when our words and arguments have no effect on him?'; 'To which of the rival claimants shall we entrust the care of this child?' The teacher is older, has more life experience and more of certain kinds of knowledge, but this does not constitute 'expertise' in such matters! His/her answer to any of these questions may be different from the children's – it is their viewpoint that carries weight, not his/hers. After all, the purpose of the drama is for them (not the teacher) to examine their thinking (not the teacher's).

Sometimes s/he will need to supply a certain amount of information, or offer the possibility of researching so that the class can discover more – but it should be only such information as the drama requires to function; often teachers, if they ask genuinely, will be surprised to find how much a class knows collectively about a topic of which teachers assume they know little. What any individual knows may be little, but the sum of what the class knows may be formidable and, if shared, can obviate the need for the teacher to tell. In any case drama, though it may use information, is not primarily about information: it is an exploration of attitudes and values, in a fictional context which has its own laws of *validity* (truth is judged by whether something is appropriate or possible or likely within that context) and *irrelevance* (on many occasions in drama the teacher may see an opportunity to teach some facts or correct some mistakes, but the criterion s/he should employ is: would this 'teaching' or 'correcting' assist, or distract from, the drama?).

It may take a while for a class to believe that the teacher is genuine in adopting the stance of 'one who does not know' instead of playing the customary teacher game of 'guess the correct answer'. They will see through the pretence if the teacher reacts enthusiastically to one suggestion: 'Good! What an interesting idea!' and coolly to another: 'Uh-huh'. It is important that the teacher is neutral and accepting in responding to all suggestions: above all that s/he is genuinely interested in, and trusting of, the children's ideas. Only so can s/he release and support them into a sense of maturity, confidence and responsibility for the quality of the work.

One of the exciting opportunities which drama offers to teachers lies in the multiplicity of registers available to them in relating to the class and in promoting learning – once they drop their monolithic stance as 'expert'. (See Chapter 11.)

A final note on the question of gaining commitment. The teacher must, as in the sample lesson opening, be serious about, and committed to, the drama if s/he is to gain belief and commitment from the children. This is so obvious that perhaps it does not need stating. Yet I have seen teachers showing condescending amusement at children's work or taking a role in a mocking way that says 'this is only a game'. Such silliness and shallowness inevitably produces silly, shallow work from the children. In this area of belief and commitment, as in many other aspects of the drama lesson (e.g. willingness to listen, to tolerate uncertainty, diversity of viewpoint and risk-taking), the teacher must act as a model for the children's behaviour. Or to cut a long story short – you must practise what you preach!

CONTEXT

In the Enquiry stage the teacher may elicit ideas from the class about what topic or theme, or what angle within the teacher's topic or theme, they are to explore in the drama. It is useful to record the ideas offered on a blackboard or similar resource, so that they are available for examination as teacher and class move from Enquiry (generating ideas) to Definition (selecting ideas). The transition between these stages is a crucial phase of the lesson. It can be helpful to have a 'ceiling' for the number of ideas offered in the Enquiry so that the subsequent selection process is not protracted.

In the Definition stage the merits of the ideas suggested are discussed, then a vote may be taken to establish a clear majority for one idea, or the 'buzz' in the class may quickly show which idea is popular without the need for a vote. Sometimes things will not be so clear-cut and suggestions may have to be combined to achieve a decision – for example where there is approximately equal support for a drama about a school and one about a youth club, what may result is a drama about a group of young people which takes place in both settings. Or if a minority are strongly in favour of an idea different to that held by the majority, the teacher might suggest that their idea could be the starting point for the next drama after this, or that their idea might be somehow folded in at a later stage in this drama. Obviously agreement isn't always easy to reach – often a minority will need to be asked to 'go with' the majority idea, sometimes the majority asked to try the minority's wishes.

Sometimes the teacher may 'classify' the suggestions in terms of their common features to aid choice. Consider, for example the following list of suggestions:

murder	'Fame' (the TV series)
Billy the Kid	bank robbery
Captain Cook	space travel

The teacher might then offer back the following 'classi-fication':

> Three of your suggestions (murder, Billy the Kid, bank robbery) are about people who commit serious crimes and put themselves outside the law. Two (Captain Cook, space travel) are about people who travel into the unknown. One ('Fame') is about people who seek to be famous.
> Which of these three kinds of situation are you interested to explore?

The list to choose from has been reduced to three instead of six, and the teacher's classification has also performed a useful service in re-casting the suggestions in a form that moves them towards a consideration of theme and attitudes or values rather than merely action.

Building the drama contract and building the drama context are inextricably linked – for the very process of elaborating the context should build the pupils' commitment to the drama.

Moving into drama can present problems for the English teacher who, valuing class discussion for its own sake, may dwell too long on the issues raised in the opening stages, forgetting that the aim is to explore the issues *in action* in a concrete fictional context. Impetus is lost, and the drama never really happens, or it becomes purposeless because the topic has been exhausted in discussion. It is not possible to lay down what length the initial discussion should be before the drama begins. Sometimes it may take only a minute or two; at other times it may be a lengthy process, but the purposes remain the same, whatever the time spent:

1 establishing a contract (or the beginnings of one);
2 creating a specific context for drama (or the beginnings of one).

Once these are sufficiently achieved there is no reason to delay moving into drama.

The drama

Here I offer a planning framework designed to enable teachers to ensure that they have all the 'ingredients' for their 'drama cake'. This framework is intended for planning both *before* and *within* the lesson – for thinking in the study and on your feet.

A PLANNING FRAMEWORK

Context

WHO is the drama about?
WHEN is it taking place?
WHERE is it set?
WHAT (broadly) is happening?

Tensions

Tension is what drives the drama. Tensions may be great or small – often great tensions are built from a succession of smaller ones; obvious or subtle – crude and obvious tensions may prepare the ground for more subtle and complex ones. Any drama will have a succession of tensions, although there may be one overriding tension that gives overall shape to the drama. There will be times in a drama when tensions aren't operating significantly, e.g. in the early stages, when roles and relationships are being built and before they are put under pressure, or times when the tension eases and the drama takes on a more elaborative or celebratory character – either rounding off a piece of work, or in preparation for the next tension.

Frame/viewpoint

The meaning we derive from a situation depends upon our viewpoint within that situation. For example, an 'incident' in a school will have a different meaning, different implications and consequences for different participants: pupil, teacher, head-teacher, parent, police, politician, etc. So the viewpoint partici-pants are asked to take on is crucial in a drama. The terms 'frame' and 'framing' (borrowed from sociology) are common-ly used in discussions about drama to mean respectively 'view-point' and 'selecting a viewpoint' within the class. When a teacher 'frames' a class, s/he determines the viewpoint or role within the drama.

Theme/learning area

Any topic we might tackle in a drama is a repository of many potential themes or learning areas. It is important to make this distinction between topic (content) and learning area – and to be clear about the learning area you are aiming for, because that decision will crucially affect your selection, presentation and sequencing of materials and activities. An example: in Journal 2, the topic or content is 'Wagon Train' but that context can be used to explore a variety of themes/learning areas: tolerance and intolerance, religious and/or racial; leadership; getting on with neighbours; coping with change and upheaval.

Focus

Drama deals with specific actions and attitudes operating in specific times and places. To begin or develop a drama a specific focus of attention and activity is required (see Figure 6).

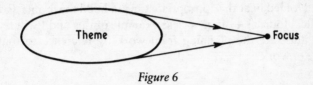

Figure 6

The initial focus needs to be selected carefully:

1 to interest the class;
2 to engage them with the theme or learning area.

As the drama develops, other foci will take the place of the initial one.

At each stage of the drama choices have to be made about:

a) Grouping
Are the class to work
as individuals?
in small groups?
as a class?

b) Conventions and modes of working
Are we to employ
mime?
tableau/still image?
hotseating?
presentation?
dramatic playing?[3]

or non-drama activities such as
discussion?
drawing?
writing?

constructing?
games/exercises?

None of these groupings or activities is better than any other; all can serve a range of specific useful functions. Often a drama will employ a wide range of groupings and conventions, each being folded in at the appropriate time to build the drama as a whole.[4] Journal 4 offers a clear example of this and I will try and illustrate the planning framework by reference to that piece of work:

Context

WHO: Poor/criminal class.
WHEN: Eighteenth century.
WHERE: London streets and Red Lion Tavern.
WHAT: One of the Red Lion fraternity is 'stopped' by another.

Tensions

OVERALL TENSIONS: living with constant fear of arrest and probable execution – not knowing who you can trust. (These are built steadily through a succession of activities.)

Frame/viewpoint

Denizens of the Red Lion Tavern. This frame does not distance: it requires direct 'living-through' engagement with the events and tensions of the play.

Theme/learning area

Honour (or lack of it) among thieves.
This is how the teacher attempted to 'realize' the framework through a succession of activities:

Activity	Grouping	Convention/mode	Focus
Session one			
1	Whole class	Discussion	Clarifying range of possible roles
2	Small group	Discussion	Allocating roles
3	Small groups within whole class activity, with possibility of interaction between groups	Discussion – physically constructing setting for scene – initial work in role (dramatic playing)	Reality of tavern setting and business of denizens
Session two			
4	Small group	Preparing and showing brief presentations of crimes	How we earn our living
5	Individual work	Mime accompanied by intermittent teacher-narration (travelling through streets to tavern)	Being alert for danger
6	As 3	As 3	As 3
7	Whole class	Discussion of historical background and examination of historical documents	Building background information
8	Individual	Writing in role: autobiography	Building individual role-identity
Session three			
9	Small group	Preparation of still image (moment of danger)	Living with danger
10	Whole class	Sharing of still images and accompanying soliloquies	Living with danger
11	Whole class	Improvised scene focused by intervention of teacher in role	a) We've been betrayed b) Calling the betrayer to account

Notes

1 For a useful discussion of contract and negotiation in the drama lesson see Neelands (1984a), Chapters 3–5.

2 See such a project outlined in Wilson and Cockcroft, Booklet Two, pp. 10–12.

3 Drama which has an ongoing, 'living through' quality. See note 4, below.

4 There isn't adequate space for me to examine in detail all the variety of drama modes. Readers might find it useful to look at the brief account of the range of modes and their 'pros and cons' given in Neelands (1984a) and at Gavin Bolton's (1979) account of dramatic playing, exercise and theatre and of how these elements can be folded in together to create a 'drama for understanding'.

JOURNAL THREE:
LORD OF THE FLIES

Drama used in relation to narrative text

- to challenge and extend pupils' perception of the significance of the narrative
- hotseating of characters from the book (represented by a 'group role') used to extend pupils' responses

Teacher role

- 'easing in'
- used to create tension (by questioning in role, attitude, use of time, pace and sequencing)
- allows very considerable pressure to be put on pupils *in role* – a quite different pressure from normal teacher pressure out of role. Pressure is possible because pupil role offers 'protection' – 'I'm being asked this as Jack, not as myself'

Opportunities for writing in role arising from the drama

I've been using drama to help with a set text. I've just finished reading *Lord of the Flies* with my fourth year CSE group. This

book doesn't raise the same difficulties as many other set texts –
it's a good read and most kids seem to get fairly easily absorbed
and moved by the story if it's taken at a reasonable pace.
Certain aspects of Golding's symbolism don't necessarily easily
mean a lot to all of them, but this doesn't really get in the way of
them enjoying the story. This group seemed to like reading the
book enormously. We got through it very fast, and when I read
the closing scenes aloud in class they were really gripped by the
narrative – even those (a fair number) who'd read on ahead by
themselves.

Successful as the book had been in the reading, when we
talked about it, there was something lacking in their response.
A lot of them appeared to be content with what seemed to me
easy answers: that, for example, things wouldn't have been so
bad on the island if Jack hadn't been there; or that what
happened, happened because they were children – adults
would have managed better. In a way they weren't able to see
this story as a statement about the human condition directly
relevant to themselves. It was still 'out there' – I wanted to try
and find a way of shifting that 'third person' stance into a 'first
person' experience.

After chatting with Maggie, I decided there were distinct
possibilities in what she calls 'hot-seating' – asking the class to
take on the roles of characters in the book and to submit to
some kind of questioning or 'interrogation' about their activities and motives. And the way the book ends left me with a
marvellous context for this to happen: once the boys had been
taken on board ship, the naval officer would surely have had to
question them to complete his report or log, and beyond that
immediate questioning would have loomed the demands of
their parents, the media and the authorities (including the
police? – if two had died?) to know what had happened on the
island. All of this would put enormous pressure on the boys. By
placing the class in role as the boys being questioned by the
officer on the warship, I hoped to exploit this built-in tension to
push them into a real and felt sense of what the boys had been

through, of what responsibility they all carried for what had happened, and of the burdens of memory and guilt it left them with. All of us know that experience of having to answer questions about actions and events we would sooner forget, if we possibly could; and by placing the class under that pressure I hoped they would identify more with the boys' experience – and see that the boys 'were' them, and all of us.

What we did occupied two lessons, the first a double, the second a single.

SESSION I (SEVENTY MINUTES)

1   I explained to the class the basic idea – that they were to be questioned 'as if' they were the boys on board ship – and asked them to get into small groups, each of which would represent one of the following characters: Ralph, Jack, Sam 'n' Eric, Roger, Maurice and Percival. (Having a group to represent one character seemed to me an odd idea at first when Maggie had suggested it. She'd said it would probably help this particular class, with many very 'shy' kids; they'd get support from each other under the pressure of the officer's interrogation and any one of the group who felt able would answer a question. This certainly proved to be right. And it had the additional advantage that we could concentrate on the main characters whose actions were fairly well documented in the novel, so the class had a fair amount of 'material' to draw on for their answers.)

2   I re-read the last few paragraphs of the book to them – to remind them of the officer's bafflement and of the boys' sense of shock when the sudden appearance of the officer brought them back with a jolt to the world they had lost (a world of childhood, and of being 'protected' by adults from the worst in themselves) and to a realization of how far they had 'fallen' since that protection had been removed. We talked a little about how each side reacted to the meeting.

3   We talked briefly about what would be likely to happen to the boys in the next few hours once they were on board ship. The class came up with: bathing, feeding, medical checks, de-lousing and general disinfection, and some attempt to clothe the boys in spare sailor's kit – they were quite amused at the thought of the boys in assorted items of uniform many sizes too large!

4   I said I would ease us into the role-play:

Well, lads, I hope you're a little more comfortable now. . . . Everything all right? . . . You've obviously had a difficult time on that island, but you'll be well looked after now. And before too long we'll have you all back home, eh? . . .

The class were seated in their groups in a rough semicircle. I went round and spoke to each 'boy', asking name, age and other straightforward bits and pieces of information. (Again I was following a 'tip' from Maggie: 'Get each group to speak to you in role in the early stages – about something neutral, just to get the feel of interacting in role with you as the officer and not as teacher.')

Right then, lads . . . well, I'm going to go and radio a report to the effect that we've picked you up off the island. Then I'll come back and see you in a bit – obviously soon I'm going to have to get a fuller report done about you and about events on the island – I'll need to know about the . . . er . . . casualties. . . . Well, see you soon.

5   Having introduced the main tension through this bit of teacher role-play, I broke out of the drama and gave the groups five minutes to prepare by considering questions such as:

What is your boy feeling like just now about the prospect of being questioned?
What things is he going to be keen to say? And what things is he *not* going to want to talk about?

They had their copies of the book, and I encouraged them to refer to the novel if they wanted to check on anything. (In the role-play that followed, too, they had their books handy and they were told they could ask for 'time out' briefly to consult with each other or consult the book if they needed to before answering a 'difficult' question. This 'pause for thought' was in fact used I think three or four times in the whole role-play.) The groups talked quietly but intently. They seemed to sense that something interesting and challenging was about to happen.

6   We moved into the role-play again, with the naval officer returning. This proved to be a very intense half-hour in which I was able to put a lot of pressure on the class within the context of the role-play. Very briefly (and omitting lots of significant detail) the stages were:

a) I asked various questions about their time on the island – but not yet about the casualties and the burning of the island. My attitude in role was that of a naval man unused to children and trying very hard to be genial with a group of 'lads', but feeling very uneasy at what was likely to be revealed. In this early part of the role-play they answered my questions about their life on the island – survival, food, shelter, etc. – with a lot of confidence and fluency.

b) I probed more with my questions: 'Things seemed to have got rather out of hand. What went wrong?'
It wasn't long before the 'Ralph' group were strongly accusing Jack of being responsible for all the trouble and in particular for Piggy's death. In the discussion that followed there seemed a very clear pattern to what the various 'boys' were saying – all were wanting to put the major blame on Jack's shoulders. The 'Jack' group, as it happened, were at one end of the semicircle and that gave me the idea for what I did next.

c) My attitude in role now was one of the utmost gravity. I said I would have to ask each of them in turn to explain what they knew of the death of Piggy. I started at the end furthest from 'Jack', so that he would be the last to make a statement – screwing up the dramatic tension steadily. All the others laid responsibility for Piggy's death, in differing proportions, with Jack and Roger. Interestingly, two people in the 'Roger' group offered different and rather contradictory defences: the first that he hadn't known that Piggy was underneath, that the rock was meant to frighten not kill; the second that he was obeying orders – Jack's.

Finally I turned to Jack – and by now the tension in the room and the pressure on the 'Jack' group were quite palpable – 'Well, Jack, what have you got to say about Piggy's death? . . .'

At that point the bell went and we had to stop – quite a cliffhanger ending! But actually I was disappointed that we'd been cut short – I'd been trying to save time for Jack, but not wanting to rush through the evidence of the other boys because of the strength of belief and involvement the class were showing.

SESSION 2 (thirty-five minutes)

1   When I tried to pick up at the point we'd left off (it was two days later) – it just didn't work. The tension we'd built couldn't easily be recalled, and when I asked 'Jack' the questions again I got virtually no response. This was a rather shy group, and in present circumstances they just clammed up. After a few minutes of trying, I gave up working on Jack in isolation – I could see that to them it felt like ordinary 'teacher pressure' for answers, not the pressure of the dramatic situation we'd had before.

2   I turned to the rest of the boys saying gravely, 'Well, there's one more casualty you haven't told me about yet. What did you say the other dead boy was called?'

My subsequent questioning about Simon's death did two things:

 a) It brought back quite a lot of tension and pressure – different to last time, but in its way just as intense.

 b) It created a significant shift in the answers, because it

wasn't possible to blame any one individual for Simon's
death – that was a shared responsibility.

My questioning came to an end in this way. In role I asked each
'boy' whether he had been among the group that had 'murdered' Simon – I used the word deliberately – and I insisted on
an answer. These answers varied from a very reluctant 'Yes', to
'Only on the edge'. When each had given their answers I
walked a few paces away and paused, shaking my head very
slowly before turning (equally slowly) to face them. Finally I
spoke: 'They're not going to believe this when I send my report.
A group of young boys . . . two boys killed . . . (a long pause).
You realize that quite apart from official reports, your parents
will have to be told? . . . Have you thought what you'll say to
them?'

A long silence followed. This was a different silence from
that earlier in the lesson when the Jack group hadn't been able
to cope with teacher pressure. It was a silence that felt right.
What *could* these boys say?

3   There was just enough time, when I eventually broke the
silence and the drama, to talk about what we'd done. There
was a strongly felt consensus among the class that it had helped
them 'get inside' the boys' situation.

It didn't occur to me at the time, but looking back I wished I
had followed this work up straight away with some writing in
role. It would have been really interesting if next lesson I'd
asked them, say, to write a letter home from the ship – how
would they have 'explained' things, how broken the news to
their parents of what their sons had been involved in, and
responsible for? Or maybe a piece of writing where one of the
boys secretly records those memories of the island that, long
after the event, won't leave him – that keep coming back in
dreams and in unguarded waking moments?

7

DRAMA AND
NARRATIVE FICTION

Most books on the teaching of English fall into one of three categories in respect to their stance towards drama:

Category one books don't mention drama at all;
Category two books say drama is 'a good thing' FULL STOP – but say little about *why* and less about *how*;
Category three books give more specific guidance, typically centering on the notion of animating text. 'If pupils act it they'll understand it better.'

In short, I think it is true to say that the most common use envisaged for drama in English classrooms by teachers of English and by writers on English teaching is that of 'acting out stories'. While I accept that one of the most obvious and helpful ways of using drama in the English classroom is alongside, or in relation to, the class reader or set text, I want to take issue with the view that this means using it merely to *animate text*. I think that such a view is simplistic and that much of the work which results from it conveys little real understanding of the text. Here I want to look a little more deeply at the relationship (both the similarities and the differences) between drama and narrative fiction.

Similarities between drama and narrative fiction

1 *Drama and fiction have in broad terms very similar purposes and procedures.* As I have already argued in Chapter 3, both seek to make explicit our implicit understandings about ourselves and the world we inhabit. And these understandings are explored through 'particular scenes where people respond directly or immediately to one another' (Jackson, 1983, 8).

2 *Both drama and fiction have as their root the experience of 'identification'.* In both we step out of the immediate circumstances of our own lives for a while and 'step into other shoes' or 'look with other eyes'. Of course the common process of identification is carried through in somewhat different ways. I think a useful way of looking at it for my present purposes is to say that the reader of fiction engages in a *private, internalized role-taking process*, whereas the drama participant *role-takes overtly and publicly*. When we employ drama as a means of looking at a book we transform that internalized role-taking which is the private world of the reader into a shared activity. (Of which more later.)

3 *Both drama and fiction require an active response from pupils.* I think that behind the use of drama to animate or enliven text is the idea that reading is somehow passive and drama active. The very idea that something needs animating or enlivening suggests that by itself it's dead or, to say the least, limp and listless! Now I won't deny that quite a lot of activity in drama lessons may be more physically active than what perhaps goes in quite a lot of English lessons, and that physical release is no bad thing in schools, where youngsters are engaged in sedentary tasks for very long periods of time. By 'active response' I am not referring to physical activity but to

the learner's mental stance towards the material s/he is working on. One can be learning actively without much or any physical activity. And it is quite possible for pupils to be physically active, yet passive as learners – I have seen not a few drama lessons where this was the case.

Drama and fiction are means which enable us to work on and examine our life experience at one remove, in an 'as if' or fictional context, in order to understand it a little better. We use words (in story) or words-and-actions (in drama) to represent, explore and organize that experience. And that requires an active stance as a learner. The English teacher's aim is what the Bullock Report calls 'responsive reading'.[1] This means that pupils ask questions of the text, and make connections between the text and their own lives. As David Jackson puts it: 'The print on the page begins to stir and come to life at the point where the reader begins to remake the text inside his own head' (1983, 15). What the English teacher tries to do is to set up what might be described as a dialogue between reader and text (see Figure 7).

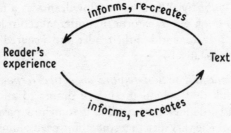

Figure 7

In his two recent books, David Jackson has usefully outlined a variety of ways in which he encourages children to be active interrogators of fictional texts, and I recommend these two books to the reader.[2]

Difficulties in looking at a work of fiction

Here I want to ask, *in what ways can drama help children to an active engagement with fictional texts?* So far, I have stressed the broad similarities or congruences between drama and story. In order to find out what drama can add to the experience of narrative fiction in the classroom, I shall have to turn to the *differences* between drama and story. But I want to approach this by way of a consideration of the obstacles which a work of fiction may present to a young reader or, to put it another way, the problems confronting a teacher teaching a work of fiction. For the teacher's task is to help young readers past their difficulties. In considering these obstacles, I shall mix two metaphors – in a way I hope is illuminating rather than confusing.

The task of the teacher in dealing with a work of fiction is essentially to enable the students to reach and make their own the key experiences or 'core' of the book (see Figure 8).

What do I mean by a book's core? I refer to those areas of human experience which are central to the book. But this does not mean simply identifying and working on the 'themes' of the book. For, as with all art, in narrative fiction content and form are interdependent – that is to say the author's treatment of certain areas of human experience is embodied in, and shaped by, the set of symbols, the language, the style and construction employed. So to come to the meaning of the book, students (and teachers) have to grapple with both content and form.

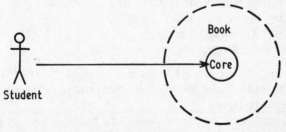

Figure 8

One common difficulty that students frequently have in dealing with a work of fiction is teacher-induced. Too often they 'can't see the wood for the trees' because the manner of treating fiction they are subjected to clogs their minds with detail, rather than allowing them to see pattern, shape, direction and overall meaning in the book. The teacher needs to find an approach which allows the student to make a 'provisional map' of the wood as soon as possible. And it may be that starting at page one and reading steadily through is *not* the way to achieve this, because that way students often don't come to making a map until they have grown weary of counting individual trees and pathways. It is possible to devise ways in which the student can be brought into contact with the core of the book right from the beginning by a selective and highly focused introduction to the material. A very well-known example is Dorothy Heathcote's treatment of *The Mayor of Casterbridge*. To oversimplify greatly, she began (more or less) at the end, not the beginning of the book, showing the class Michael Henchard's will and asking them what could have produced so strong a wish 'that no man remember me'.[3]

Sometimes mapping a wood means getting past barriers and obstacles. Like a wood, a book may have barriers round it, or obstacles littered through it. Common ones (particularly in the later stages of secondary school) are:

remoteness (or apparent remoteness) of the events and context of the book from the lives of the readers;
'difficult' and/or outmoded language;
'difficult' use of symbols;
'difficult' style of construction;
sheer size and length.

If the students are to reach the core of the book, the teacher will have to find ways of helping them over, round or through the barriers (see Figure 9).

Journal 1 offers a clear example of a teacher identifying the barriers presented by a particular novel, Rosemary Sutcliff's

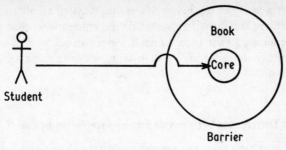

Figure 9

Dragon Slayer, and devising a highly selective way in to the text that enabled them to make provisional maps of the material very quickly, and to adopt an active, enquiring stance towards the book. Also see the article, 'Wizard of Earthsea: a way in through drama', by David Eccles (1984, 67).

Sometimes a book will present no obvious barriers. It is generally straightforward at the narrative level, a good read, and students feel at home with characters and plot without undue trouble. But their reading is really surface reading. There is more to the book than they have reached. They have stopped short of the core (see Figure 10).

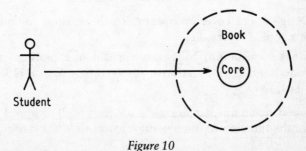

Figure 10

In this case, the teacher needs to find ways of amplifying or challenging the initial responses of the students, so that they can penetrate to the core. Journal 3 gives an account of work designed to do this with a fourth year group studying *Lord of the Flies*.

Differences between drama and narrative fiction

So, my argument runs, there are certain difficulties which teacher and learner may encounter in looking at a fictional text – difficulties which drama may be able to help with. That help is available because drama, although sharing considerable common ground with narrative fiction, is different in certain key respects and can therefore add something to the treatment of fictional text in the classroom. Quite simply, *because drama as an art form works in certain crucial respects differently from narrative as an art form, it distorts the material or subject matter differently, illuminates it differently and so can produce another way of seeing the people, situations, tensions and dilemmas in the story*. And the process of translating material from one art form to another often compels close attention to the original in order to ensure that the transfer is valid and soundly based. David Jackson offers two examples of translating narrative fiction into visual art forms as a means of enabling children to explore, or express their understanding of, the meaning of the original narrative:

Design a book cover which expresses the meaning and spirit of a book (*Nancenuke*)

Make a cartoon or collage as a means of exploring your understanding of a narrative poem (*Prince Kano*). (1983, 70–3, 78–83)

I would maintain that drama is uniquely well-equipped to serve the function of 'illumination by transfer' for narrative fiction, because drama and narrative share so much common ground that the differences which do exist are particularly useful for sharpening our perceptions and insights about the narrative.

So what are the differences between drama and narrative? James Moffett gives us a good start in looking at them:

> The action of a narrative is not ongoing, it *has* gone on; it is *reported* action. As such it is a résumé of some previous drama – summarized and abstracted by *somebody*, a reporter, narrator. Although grammar tells us that the difference between *what is happening* and *what happened* is a time difference, much more than time is involved. Tense is a relation of speaker to events: if the events are unrolling before his eyes – ongoing – they are being coded for the first time by someone who is *attending* them (or 'assisting at' them, as the French say) and who is therefore in the same plane of reality as the act-ors. This is his point of view. His coding of events is a first-order abstraction. As a report of what happened, narrative is a second-order abstraction.
>
> Compare the sensory stream of someone watching a football game with the Sunday newspaper account of the same game. Narrative is a further abstraction of some observer's prior abstraction. What makes events past is reporting them. What makes events present is attending them. Whereas narrative summarizes drama, drama elaborates narrative. Consider a reviewer's recapitulation of a play performance, then a dramatization of a short story. Whether actual or artifactual, drama is *what is happening*, with all that this implies. (1968, 62)

In the chart overleaf, I have tried first to summarize Moffett's thinking on the differences between drama and narrative, and then to point to some of the consequences that follow from those differences.

Narrative	Drama
What has happened	*What is happening*
Second-order abstraction (mediated to us by another).	First-order abstraction (unmediated by another; we are present at it).
Summarizes drama.	Elaborates narrative.
Difference in viewpoint	
Involves a private relationship between reader and fiction.	Its interactive nature means participants have a shared, public relationship with the fiction.
The reader's viewpoint is selected for him by the writer, who mediates the fiction to him.	Operating directly upon (being present at) the fictional events, participants can select their viewpoint.
Different use of sign	
Operates through a single sign system (written text).	Uses multiple sign systems in combination.
Different use of time	
Tends towards linear, sequential development – onward movement of events.	Dwells in the present moment.

DIFFERENCE IN VIEWPOINT

When I read a novel, my viewpoint upon its events and interactions is that given to me by the novelist. It may be the viewpoint of a single character; it may be a multiple viewpoint, so that I 'see with the eyes' of several characters; or, it may be the authorial 'overview'. Whichever, it is selected for me by the writer who is mediating/reporting the action of the novel to me. As a reader, I experience a private relationship with the writer and his fiction, seeing the fictional events from the vantage point(s) he offers me.

If I am one of a group engaged in a dramatic exploration of the material in the same book, I would be operating upon it in significantly different ways. Drama is a social, interactive activity – in drama ideas are developed and crystallized in groups; individual ideas and viewpoints are tested, modified and built upon, through interaction. So the engagement with the fictional material is shared and public rather than individualized and private. This means that there is a tendency for multiple viewpoints to emerge. And because we are dealing directly with the events (we are present at them, rather than having them mediated to us by another) we do not need to accept the viewpoint the writer has selected. We can explore any of the viewpoints implicit in the narrative. For example, in *Lord of the Flies* we might choose to try and see events through the eyes of Percival Wemyss Madison and the other littl'uns rather than from the viewpoint of Jack, Ralph and Piggy.

Put another way, operating in a drama mode allows us to elaborate narrative and to expand our apprehensions of the entire pattern of events, attitudes, behaviours and interactions which the narrative represents selectively. To use Moffett's term, we have converted a second-order abstraction back into a first-order abstraction; in a sense we have reversed the writer's process of selection, to look directly at the web of meaning and interaction s/he has 'abstracted from' to construct a narrative. Of course, in a sense, this is what the experienced reader is doing all the time in his or her head as s/he reads a novel. S/he 'reads between the lines', conjures up events, attitudes, interactions and viewpoints which the book only hints at or touches upon. The inexperienced reader may need a lot of help with this process of elaboration (of 'remaking' the novel in his or her own head), and it can help greatly to externalize the process, to make it public and shared. Indeed, I would argue that experienced readers, too, can have their understanding of a novel expanded or deepened in this way.

I want now to try and summarize this section by using a metaphor. Let us suppose that we have read a novel and explored the fiction in the book through a dramatic exploration. We can think of the fictional experience which we have operated upon as a 'web of meaning' (comprising people, attitudes, behaviour, interactions, reflections, settings, etc.). In reading the novel we find that the writer has selected certain strands of the web as a representation or report of that experience. In the drama exploration we find ourselves placed within the whole web of meaning and although we will still look or experience selectively, it is less selective than through the writer's report, because we can experience any of the strands we choose and we encounter them directly rather than as mediated to us by the writer.

I want now to dwell a little on the implications of the phrase I used a few lines ago: 'within the whole web of meaning', and particularly upon that word *within*. I have talked of making the private experience of the individual reader into a public and shared experience (through the use of drama) so that the reader may be helped to remake the experience of the narrative in his or her head. Of course, good English teachers try to do this anyway.

The class novel offers opportunities for 'experience shared among a group in which the joint response enriches the varying individual responses' (Sharp, 1980, 76). David Jackson's writings offer many examples of pupils sharing their responses to a story with each other through discussion work of various kinds. What drama allows us to do, that discussion methods do not, is to *share responses or make shared meanings within the fiction*. In discussion we can share outside viewpoints about the experiences of Piggy, Ralph, and Jack, and others on the island; through drama, through role-taking, we can look *with their eyes* and experience the clash of their attitudes and wills *from the inside*. In discussion we can relate the experiences of the people in the book to our own experiences, but sometimes – if the material is sensitive – that can be threatening. We are not always ready or willing to open up our experiences and feelings to the inspection of others. Through drama we can explore situations or dilemmas analogous to those in the book, and make connections in our minds between the two fictions, and we have the protection of a fiction in our exploration of issues from the book – the material is distanced and therefore less threatening, because we are looking not at *our* attitudes but at *theirs* (the people whose roles we have adopted). Of course we *are* exploring our own responses, but at one (protected) remove.

DIFFERENT USE OF SIGN

All art operates through significant use of sign. But each art form is distinguished by the kinds and combination of sign it employs. I have already touched upon the difference in this respect between narrative and drama when I said that one uses words and the other words-and-actions to explore our life-experience. I want to look more precisely at that difference.

Narrative fiction operates through only one kind of sign – written words on a page. Through this form or sign it *reports* or *describes* selectively 'what has happened'. Drama by contrast, *demonstrates* 'what is happening'. Participants and spectators experience the events of drama in the *now*, as we experience life itself, and that experience, like life itself, operates on the level of multiple sign. Words do not stand alone, but are uttered through sound, accompanied by other (non-verbal) sounds, broken by silence, enmeshed in movements; movements are broken by stillness, and take place in space in relation to other people and objects, which may be placed or adorned or lit or obscured in a multiplicity of ways. For readers who are experiencing difficulty with the single sign system of the written text, the multiple sign system of drama can offer a powerful way of gaining access to the fiction. They can re-create the world of the text using all the familiar signing resources they employ in their everyday lives and interactions. For drama is of all the arts the one which most resembles life, and our everyday interactions, most closely. It is the most concrete, least abstracted of the arts. Narrative fiction abstracts to a greater degree than drama from the flux of everyday experience:

1 it operates at a greater distance from events – THEN rather than NOW;

2 it has selected only one sign system (words on a page) to 'describe' those events.

Dance represents a different kind, or direction, of abstraction from drama. It remains like drama in 'now' time, but has excluded words from its range of signing.

I have already said that drama allows us to elaborate narrative in the sense of making explicit the many viewpoints implicit in it; here I am arguing that drama allows us to elaborate upon narrative text in a different (though closely linked) sense – it allows us to employ the whole range of signing systems which are available to us as human beings to explore the meaning of the words on the page.

I want to add one rider to my argument that drama is 'life-like'. It is, in an important sense, both like and unlike everyday life:

Like   in that it employs the same rich variety of signing;
Unlike in that it is shaped, being a representation of real
         experience, rather than a real experience as such.

An important consequence is that whereas happenings in real life have a random quality, and we do not expect all happenings and signs to have significance, we do expect them all to be significant in drama, because they have been selected, consciously or unconsciously and placed in a context where we expect them to mean. An anecdote by Groucho Marx illustrates the point nicely. He watched the scratches on Julie Harris's legs intently during a performance of *I am a Camera*:

At first we thought this had something to do with the plot and we waited for these scratches to come to life. But . . . it was never mentioned in the play and we finally came to the conclusion that either she had been shaving too close or she'd been kicked around in the dressing room by her boyfriend.

                                                              (Elam, 1980, 9)

Eventually Marx decided that the scratches were nothing to do with the play, but rather an intrusion from the randomness of real life. His waiting 'for the scratches to come to life' is eloquent testimony to the assumption in drama that every detail, however small, is an intentional sign. So drama allows us to use all the rich resources of real-life signing, but makes us attend to them in a special manner, expecting that they will convey significant meanings. Young people are, generally speaking, stronger at reading action, or words-embedded-in-action, than they are at reading words alone. Drama allows them to explore these strengths in a highly focused way.

DIFFERENT USE OF TIME

Narrative fiction describes 'what has happened'. The writer mediates the experience to us; in order to do so he describes a sequence of events. In that sequence the unfolding of events, their onward movement – the question, 'what happened next?' – tends to be central in the reader's mind. Drama demonstrates 'what is happening', and we experience the event directly: we are present at it. Its tendency is to dwell in the present moment, rather than to attend to the onward movement of events. Past and future are important, but important in so far as they impinge on the present. Its concern is situation, rather than story. Therefore it gives us an opportunity to think round a situation, to see it from different points of view, to tease out its meaning, in a way that the onward movement of narrative fiction does not always allow. 'Whereas narrative summarizes drama, drama elaborates narrative.' (Moffett, 1968, 62.)

We may decide to re-run or re-work a situation, to devise a variety of ways of exploring it, or to arrest the action at certain moments of time and create a tableau or still image to convey our understanding of that moment's significance. In all of these ways we may spend a considerable time examining only a few moments of action, because we are dwelling in situation rather than moving on in story. Such a way of working has considerable potential for probing into the meaning of narrative text. Not only does the pace at which we operate within the drama help us to 'elaborate narrative', but we also have the resource of the reflection which occurs as we step out of the drama to consider its shaping and its meanings. Some drama approaches – notably those in my category B of the strategies described in the next section – have built into their very perspective a strong element of reflection, because they allow 'distance' from the material, given by the viewpoint from which the events and characters are being examined. The various viewpoints suggested in category B will each have their own purposes and generate their own questions – will employ a different 'microscope' for examining the text.

Strategies

What follows is a broad classification of the variety of drama strategies a teacher can employ to work on narrative text. It seems to me that they fall into three broad categories (which overlap to some extent):

A) Using role to step into the events of the book and into the shoes of the characters.
B) Framing the class to consider the book's events from viewpoints other than those of character or reader.
C) Working by analogy.

I want to spend a little time considering each of them.

A) STEPPING INTO THE BOOK'S EVENTS AND THE CHARACTERS' SHOES THROUGH ROLE

What may seem the most obvious and straightforward kind of strategy is in fact in some ways the most problematic. Way back in 1967 John Allen warned about the difficulties:

For children to make the Polyphemus story, for example, really 'their own' . . . is more difficult than to invent their own story because they have to work within the precise form that is laid down by the original chain of events . . . the belief expressed from time to time that children can come closer to a story by acting it rather than simply listening to it is not always borne out in practice.[4]

We have in effect come full circle – to my opening remarks on p. 66 on using drama to 'animate text'. The problem resides in the fact that if in drama we are working on a given narrative sequence whose development and outcome are already known, that tends to pull us towards concentration on 'getting the plot right', on 'what happens next', on the momentum of events and plot. We are not submitting to a dramatic experience, only representing an experience (of reading a story) we have already had; our representation will tend to be condensed and allusive, rather than elaborative as in a genuine drama mode. It is difficult to see what is added by such enactment. If teachers are to use drama to work upon the material in a narrative text, then it is essential that the work is geared to preserve the distinctive dynamic of drama – dwelling in *situation* rather than moving on in *story*. This might mean, for example, that the teacher:

Sets up dramatic explorations of incidents which are only briefly sketched or hinted at, rather than fully described, in the book, so that the sense of being tied to a detailed narrative sequence or set of outcomes is less strong;
Or
asks the class to work in drama upon incidents fully described in the book before they have read them, or when they have only begun to read them. Thus the class can explore how they think a momentous scene will develop before they find out how the author treats it;
Or
invents incidents (or asks the class to invent incidents) that do not occur in the book at all, but might have;

Or

re-casts the manner of treating events in the book so they are 'freed' from the narrative drive of the story: for example, students in role as characters from the book might be asked to recall its events for the sake of a court of inquiry; or to explain events to, and comfort, the family of a dead character; or to tell (or represent to) a psychiatrist the dreams that keep coming back to them about that time. The work on *Lord of the Flies* in Journal 3 is of this kind, where the boys were asked to recall events on the island, so that the naval officer could make his report. Here we are beginning to move into category B.

B)   FRAMING THE CLASS TO CONSIDER THE EVENTS IN THE BOOK FROM VIEWPOINTS OTHER THAN THAT OF THE READER OR OF A CHARACTER IN THE BOOK

For example, as:

A court of inquiry, or inquest.
Historians or archaeologists deciphering source material (the book, or fragments of it) about past events (see Journal 1).
Police (or other authorities) investigating a crime or suspicious events.
Friends or relations of the characters.
Spiritual mediums able to communicate with one, some or all of the dead characters.
Counsellors/confidants/advisers to the characters.
Psychologists, social workers or other professionals appointed to help the characters.

(These are but a few of the many options available.)

Framing the students in ways like these means that the problem of the narrative pulling against the drama (or vice versa) is dispensed with. The students are not being asked to re-create the events in the book through drama, but to enquire into, and perhaps intervene in, these events. Thus the activity is less obviously dramatic, but it can have its own built-in tension. And re-creation through drama can have a place within the enquiry/intervention mode. For example, a group of historians might reconstruct past events as they had worked them out from the small fragments of a document recently discovered (fragments of the text suitably presented by the teacher). Or a court of inquiry might want a reconstruction of events. Or a psychologist might give the character a chance to role-play an event and then try it another way, to practise coping better with life-pressures. In each case the overall frame within which the re-enactment takes place gives it an orientation such that narrative drive does not predominate.

c) WORKING BY ANALOGY

Drama can be used to assist the student's experience of a narrative text without ever dealing with the content of the book directly in drama. Sometimes a more indirect approach can be useful, whereby the teacher selects for exploration through drama a problem and context which have clear parallels with the book. Through the drama issues are raised, problems tackled, tensions felt which can amplify the student's understanding of the book as s/he reads it, recognizing the parallels and comparing the responses in the drama to those of the characters in the book. When a class and teacher are working by analogy to illuminate a text, the drama work can follow its own laws and dynamic – there is no contrary pull from the narrative text. All the teacher has to ensure is that in planning and shaping the drama s/he is focusing it clearly towards those areas of experience s/he wishes to examine. The choices the students make in developing the work must be within that clear framework. But working through analogy does make particularly stringent demands on the teacher to be clear about the core experiences or themes in the book s/he wishes to examine, otherwise the analogy simply will not strike home.

In a way I am unhappy about categorizing the ways of using drama on narrative fiction as I have done. For there is overlap, as I have briefly pointed out, and there are approaches which do not fit neatly into any of the three categories. For example, the work described in Journal 4 does not employ the events and characters from *Smith*, nor does it remove the theme tackled (honour, or lack of it, among thieves) to an analogous context. It occupies instead a sort of middle ground between categories A and C. The context (the tavern and its denizens) and the dilemmas (betrayal and fear of capture) are very close to, though not identical with, those in the book. David Eccles's work on *A Wizard of Earthsea* (1984), alternated between employing the broad context of a 'School for Wizards' and looking specifically at events, characters and problems dealt with in the book itself. Perhaps it would be more appropriate to speak of orientations rather than categories; I am not sure. *I think the most important consideration is that the teacher should think carefully about the kind of approach most suitable for the particular book s/he is dealing with, and the purposes for which s/he is using drama.*

Is the aim to get the class over some initial barriers, to create an appropriate 'mental set' for beginning work on the book? Is it to amplify their understanding of the themes, events, characters, and style of the book, as they read it?
Or is it to consolidate, deepen or challenge their understanding once they have finished reading the text?
Is the drama 'a way in' to a better understanding of the book, in which case the drama will be a means to another end?
Are reading the book and doing drama parallel activities where each feeds the other in roughly equal measure?
Or is the book primarily a springboard for other activities — including drama — because it raises interesting issues to be

tackled through talking, role-playing and writing, rather than because of the inherent quality of the book itself. Andrew Brennan and Sue Llewellyn describe a project of this kind, (1984, 88), where Marjorie Darke's *A Question of Courage* was used to trigger some drama work on issues of gender, both in the historical context of the suffrage movement and in the present day.

Notes

1 *A Language for Life*, HMSO, 1975, p. 128.
2 *Continuity in Secondary English* (1982) and *Encounters with Books* (1983).
3 For an account of the project see Wagner (1979) pp. 188–9.
4 *Drama*, DES Education Survey 2, HMSO, 1967, p. 10.

8

WORKING
ON PLAYTEXT

I have argued against the practice of 'acting out' scenes from
novels. Playtext is, however, written to be 'acted out'. Unlike
narrative text, dramatic text is incomplete until it is realized in
action. So part of the process of examining a playtext in the
English classroom is likely to be concerned with enacting
portions of the text in order to understand the play better. The
emphasis on *understanding* is important – and it is best if the
teacher establishes clearly that, when pupils are enacting scenes
or watching such an enactment, the purpose is not to demonstrate acting skills, but to share understandings about the text.
It may well be that for some classes enacting scenes from the
text is still threatening. Here the kind of procedures outlined in
Journal 6, where 'spectators' in fact direct the 'actors', may
offer appropriate and necessary protection. Working on tableaux or still images of crucial moments in the play offers less
threat than naturalistic enactment. It also has the advantage of
assisting the class to attend to the significant detail of a
dramatic encounter, in a way that 'rolling' enactment may not.
And the process of selecting crucial moments and of justifying

the selection is one that can be very helpful in developing understanding of a play.

Re-creating scenes from a playtext is one way of coming to understand it better. But it will need to be used selectively, alongside other approaches. All the drama strategies outlined earlier as suitable for use with narrative fiction can be used on playtext too. Here is a brief outline in note form of some of the varied strategies one teacher employed when working on *Romeo and Juliet* with a third year class. A fuller account of the project appears elsewhere (see Bailey, 1984).

Phase one: the way in

Aim: To avoid initial reactions of 'Oh, no, not Shakespeare!' To move class into working on the play without knowing they were, by creating a dramatic context whose elements were close to those in the play. Once pupils were 'hooked' by that work the bridge to the text could be crossed.

Activities:

a) Stage-fighting: controlled game-like physical activity – first in pairs, then pairs divided to make two opposing gangs.

b) Establishing a context for the fight – gangs named and identities and causes of conflict elaborated through discussion and in-role interview (reporter).

c) Build-up to the fight elaborated, and fight re-created. Teacher as authority figure (military commander) intervenes in role and threatens death penalty if any repetition.

d) Two gangs hold separate 'conferences' about the edict.

Phase two: working direct on the text

Activities:

a) Text given to class and Act I, Scene I read and discussed. (Much appreciation of the bawdy humour.) Then a film of the scene, to the Duke of Verona's arrival, played to class. Discussion of reasons for the conflict, whether Duke's ban will work, drawing many parallels with 'gang context' established earlier.

b) Class hotseat Romeo and Juliet (played by pupils) about their plan to marry secretly, interrogating them about potential implications and effects of their plan.

c) Role-plays in pairs: Juliet–Nurse; Romeo–Friar. Former persuading latter to co-operate with plan to marry secretly.

d) Pupil asked: 'What would have happened if the Friar had told the families about the marriage?' Class were keen to explore this possibility through drama.

Whole group role-play: Friar summons both families to the Church as their religious adviser, in order to persuade them to allow the marriage.

e) Groups of four work on Act III, Scene 4 (death of Mercutio and Tybalt):

   i) read scene and work out sequence of events;
   ii) prune text to a barebones version – nothing essential omitted;
   iii) enact pruned scene to class;
   iv) create and enact a modern analogy to the scene.

Phase three: review

Activities:

a) Whole group scene created where bodies of Romeo and Juliet were brought before the Duke (as in Zeffirelli film). Teacher, as Duke, paraphrases and expands Duke's speech, insisting all bear a responsibility. All present are asked, one by one, to speak out loud their thoughts and feelings on the occasion.

b) A court of inquiry (not a trial) – where does responsibility for the deaths lie? Tybalt, Mercutio, Paris, are 'revived' for this purpose. Pairs of pupils appointed to be key characters and their legal representatives:

   i) several lessons spent researching text to prepare background and evidence;

ii) teacher, as Duke, interviews each pair, unsympatheti-
cally, pressuring – a kind of rehearsal for the inquiry;

iii) court is held – pupils as chairpersons, jury and
witnesses.

Readers may find it useful to refer to two other accounts of
using drama approaches to playtext in the English classroom:
Peim and Elmer (1984) and O'Neill (1983).

9
JOURNAL FOUR:
SMITH

Drama working broadly 'in parallel' with reading of narrative text

- also creating opportunities for language work – spoken and written

Building belief through slow, careful elaboration of dramatic context and role

- choice of appropriate early focus (living with fear of capture) for later work (treachery among thieves)
- teacher talk, in setting up a drama task, used carefully to draw attention to detail, and to structure the work by offering class clear options (e.g. walking back to the Red Lion)

Teacher role

- used early on to support unobtrusively from the fringes of the drama (landlord)

- used later to inject specific tension and dilemma (news of Toby's capture)

Finding a direction 'within' the drama

- difference between third person thinking and first person 'now-time' drama thinking
- use of teacher role and 'theatre' sign/symbols to focus drama or move it forward, create tension, bring in contributions from more people, etc., from *within* the drama

I want to push a bit further with drama work than I've gone so far – I'm getting quite excited about the possibilities, but I'm conscious at the moment that what I've done so far has been limited:

1 Apart from some work with 1S, it's been tied very closely to getting kids to move into and understand a book better – I've had very specific and tight purposes, and that was reassuring when I was moving into what was, for me, a totally new way of working. Now I'd like to branch out a bit. I still want to work the drama in connection with class readers because they give me my material ready-made. At the moment I'm very unsure of how to plan a drama 'in vacuo', as the lesson on 'The Way West' showed. But the *Lord of the Flies* work, particularly, gave me a strong sense of the value the role-play had *in itself*. That fourth year group surprised me, and I think surprised themselves. I was intrigued by the quality of the response from many of them – and how, as the naval officer, I was able to elicit responses from them in a quite different way than I can as teacher.
2 However, as the naval officer (and as Curator of the British Museum), I was still very like teacher in many ways: all the controls were in my hands; I was at the centre of things; interaction and discussion was all through me. Listening to Maggie talking about her use of role, it's obvious that she often uses roles that give much more responsibility to the

class. Although I'm scared about where this might lead I want to try something that helps get me moving in this direction.

I'm a little way into reading *Smith* by Leon Garfield with my other second year class (2F), and I think it offers possibilities for working in the ways I want to try. The book is a vivid account of a young boy's life in, and final escape from, the underworld of eighteenth-century London. It's not an easy book, given its language and imagery, for a class such as this (although they're officially 'mixed ability', a large number of them, in conventional classroom work, seem very limited in their language – both oral and written). I have in mind something like this: to create a drama in which the class become the denizens of the Red Lion Tavern in London that Smith knew. We won't be working with the *events* of the book at all, but with its *general atmosphere*: trying to create a sense of that subculture of the London poor/criminal world of the time, where many had no option but crime if they were to survive, where you could be hanged for stealing a handkerchief as easily as for killing a man, and where fear of the gallows was a condition of life. This can go on *in parallel* with our reading of the book, and I think and hope both should complement and reinforce each other. And – very important – I'm hoping that the drama will stimulate some interesting talking and writing.

SESSION ONE (thirty-five minutes)

Overall aim: 'edging into' the drama:

1 creating the context;
2 defining the roles.

Sequence

1 *Explanation*:
We are going to see if we can 'step into the shoes' of the in-habitants of the Red Lion Tavern, not re-creating the events of

the book, but making our own version of what might happen to such people. (Note: I didn't call what we were doing 'drama' – in fact in the drama work I've done so far, it's gone best when I haven't used the word 'drama'. The word seems to have meanings for a lot of kids which are irrelevant to the kind of work I'm trying to do.)

2 *Discussion*:

About the kind of people in the tavern, and about how they got their living – we made a list of the kinds of crime we'd seen mentioned in the book. I broke the list down into a classification as follows:

a) People who occasionally/intermittently steal, as need arises, to keep body and soul together.

b) Regular petty criminals.

c) 'Big-time' criminals – I insisted that there would be only be one or two 'High Tobies' (highwaymen), as in the book, and that the rest would be less spectacular, small-time criminals. I included the 'fence', or 'receiver', that one boy had suggested in this category – a person at the centre of many other's crimes.

3 *Selection of roles*:

I asked 2F to get into small groups (anything from two to six) and each group to decide how they got their living. Result: a couple of highwaymen; two 'receivers'; three groups of 'footpads'; two groups of pickpockets, one specializing in handkerchiefs.

4 *Establishing the context*:

We spent a while discussing the look, sound and smell of the tavern, and its layout, and how we could set it up in the classroom. Then I asked them (still in groups) to establish the places they normally sat at in the tavern: 'Do you want to draw attention to yourselves by sitting somewhere prominent? Or do you want to keep out of sight – in a corner, perhaps in shadows away from the light of the oil-lamps?' Most set up their tavern tables round the fringes of the room, except notably the 'receivers' who held court near the bar (teacher's desk).

Next I said we would move into the tavern 'as if' we were its regular inhabitants: 'We'll start fairly early in the evening. Decide whether you are already there, or not yet at the tavern – you may come as a group, or separately and meet up at the tavern, whichever suits best. I don't know what business you've got at the tavern that night: you may be going to sell or "exchange" something you've acquired; or you may be going to find information – who's away from home and "burglar-able", who's likely to travel alone and along which path; or just to meet your associates and exchange gossip; or perhaps to plan tomorrow's activities. Right, let's begin, and don't forget, whoever you are in the tavern, that you always have to be on your guard – that one false move could mean the gallows.'

This began well – the children talked secretively at tables, or sidled in and there was for a little while an 'atmosphere', but soon I noticed that two or three thefts had occurred *within the tavern*. I let it ride, hoping they would get past that soon, but then when a 'mugging' began, I decided enough was enough. I stopped the drama (the lesson was nearly at an end anyway) and tried to explain that the criminal activities would take place *outside* the tavern. The Red Lion, I said, was a refuge for them all, and while they might well not trust many of the people there, it was unlikely that wholesale mutual robbery and assault would be going on. I had no time, hurried my explan-ation, and didn't get the sense that 2F were listening anyway. My plan was in pieces!

Maggie's Verdict:
'It sounds to me as if you've got them excited at the thought of "being" criminals, then put them in a context (the Red Lion) where in your view they're not supposed to commit crimes – so the kids have decided they'll commit them anyway. I guess you'll have to go back in order to go forwards. Let them have their crimes, then go back to the tavern – it may be that they

come then with a clearer sense of their roles and of the place as a "refuge" and as "HQ".'

My Response: 'But if I let them act out crimes it'll be chaotic, won't it?'

Maggie: 'Maybe. . . .'

SESSION TWO (seventy minutes)

Overall aim: as for Session one.

Sequence

1 After clearing desks to the side I asked the groups to create *very* brief scenes (ten seconds maximum – I counted out 10 seconds to fix that time in their mind) to show the rest of us how they earn their living – 'so we get a clearer idea of all the people in the tavern'. I gave them two minutes only to prepare their scenes. 'Keep it simple. Keep it clear.' I was keen to keep this early part of the work on a tight rein. I didn't want them to have a lot of time to elaborate on thefts and assaults:

a) I didn't want things to get 'out of control'.

b) I'm uneasy (ethically) about getting kids to actually *enact* scenes of violence – I'm not sure what it does to them, but my instincts tell me it's not good. Hence the very strict time pressure, the formality of showing, and the neutrality of purpose (spreading information around).

The scenes showed various street and highway robberies and pickpocketings (including one very 'nifty' routine by a group of six girls – a handkerchief was deftly removed from a pocket, and within seconds had passed through several pairs of hands so that it was rapidly lost in a crowd and separated from the original pickpocket).

2 'So, the people who frequent the Red Lion are obviously skilled at what they do – they have to be to succeed and to

escape detection. They live on their wits, constantly looking over their shoulders. . . . Can we now suppose that, having committed your crime, your gang split up and make their way through the streets separately to a place of safety – say the Red Lion. After a job it's safer to all go by different routes.

'I know there's not a lot of space here, but can everybody get into a space as far as they can from other people, and in a minute do your journey back to the tavern? It may be at night so you can use the shadows to hide you. It may be daytime so you may use the crowds to hide you. Do you sneak there? Or walk boldly along? I don't know, but I guess that, whenever or however, your eyes and ears will be on the alert for the slightest signal of danger. When you're ready, make a start.'

They responded eagerly to this obvious tension – by and large managing to ignore each other. I let it go on a minute or so, before shouting, quite loudly, 'Oy, you!' This made many of them jump and exclaim, then when they saw the grin on my face, they sighed, laughed and jabbered with relief. I broke the drama immediately and we sat and talked briefly about the nervous tension and strain of living constantly on the watch.

3 We went back to the tavern and did again what I had attempted last lesson, with two differences:

   a) I explained before we started that the tavern was a place of refuge for all its customers and that, 'while you may not like or trust everybody there (after all, some had been known to sell their fellows to the gallows for the price of a drink) and who knows whether they might rob each other outside its walls – nevertheless within the Red Lion, there is a code, an agreement, for all have a common need for refuge, for companionship and for time to plan and deal'.

   b) I took the role of landlord (as last time, but used it more definitely now). This enabled me to greet most of them as

they came in, and to help their seriousness by my seriousness: to establish a number of interactions and deals ('I
hear tell you got a fine collection of handkerchiefs today,
Sarah. . . . oh never you mind how I know (*winking*). . . .
Well that fellow there (*pointing*), it just so happens, was
asking me about buying some handkerchiefs, so it might
be to your advantage to. . . .'); to create atmosphere (by
being obtrusively nosy about people's business as I collected tankards and orders from the tables, and by
making remarks such as, 'Somebody come lookin' for
you this afternoon, Sam. . . . No, don't know him . . .
seemed keen to get in touch though. Had a mean, angry
look in his eye – somebody you've double-crossed, eh?
I'd sit by the back door if I were you, maybe. . . .'); and
generally to support the class in role.

This time the atmosphere of quiet, watchful conversation
and secretive dealing was sustained for quite a long time –
not far off ten minutes – and when I stopped the drama, 2F
seemed genuinely pleased with what they'd managed to
create. 'It just felt real in the tavern', one girl said.

4 I thought that this would be a useful point to introduce some
written work. What I wanted was an autobiographical
statement in role – an account from each of them of their
background, life, way of earning a living and thoughts about
their future. We spent the remaining half of the lesson
talking in a fairly wide-ranging way about eighteenth-
century London – its physical feel and look, the lives of its
poor and criminal classes, its cheap gin, its no-go areas for
the Bow Street runners, its gaols and the general reliance on
severity of sentencing rather than probability of detection.
We were able to draw quite a lot of information from *Smith*
itself, but I had also borrowed a few short extracts from
relevant documents from the History Department: a final
statement by a woman hanged for petty theft; a list of people
hanged in one calendar year, and of their crimes; an account
of the diet of the London poor; and a vivid description of a

London street and its occupants. I passed copies of these around for them to browse through, feeling that in this way the material might inform their writing rather than 'clog' it with lots of facts.

They did the writing for homework, and I was quite pleased with what they achieved: some had obviously drawn on *Smith*, and wrote of having to fend for themselves from an early age – some had been abandoned by their parents; a couple wrote that their mothers had been hanged when they were young. Most gave an account of their criminal life that felt basically authentic – with a few excursions into vivid fantasy or anachronism. On the whole I certainly felt the writing, as well as being a useful exercise in itself, had helped confirm their sense of identity with their chosen role in the drama.

SESSION THREE (seventy minutes)

The next lesson was to be the one where I took the plunge. I was going to try using role in a way which allowed the class to take more responsibility, and to operate more flexibly, try 'thinking on my feet' instead of having everything worked out in advance.

The plan was as follows:

1 Groups to create a still picture of a moment where a crime went wrong and put them in danger of capture. We look at each in turn and I put my hand on the shoulder of one or two figures in each picture to speak aloud what is going through their minds at that moment.
   Aim: to recall and reinforce the sense of insecurity of the lives of denizens of the Red Lion.

2 Back to the tavern after this unnerving incident. Before this scene begins, warn them that after a while I will enter in role as somebody else, not the landlord. Because I felt insecure about it, and because I knew the words needed to be selected

carefully, I had written my initial 'script' and learnt it by heart!

'(*Rushing in.*) Give me a drink somebody, quick. (*Loud, urgent. Then pause.*) We're all done for now – you, me, the lot of us. They've arrested Toby. One of you shopped him. . . . I was close by – hiding – I heard them talking about our informer. Toby knows he was shopped. He knows all our secrets. If I know Toby, it won't be long before he shops us – "If I'm to hang, they can come with me," he'll say. . . . (*Pause. Long look round at every member of the group, before. . . .*)

It was you!'

(I had selected in advance a strong, confident boy – David – to accuse – someone I thought could cope with the role.)

I also had this available in case some or all of the class didn't take my role seriously enough:

'You won't laugh when they come for you – and they will!'

3 After letting things run on a very little while after my accusation, stop the drama and:

a) check that David is happy to continue as the accused;

b) ask if anyone would be willing to take over my role.

Then re-run the accusation and see how things develop – and hope I will be quick-witted enough to cope!

This session would bring me to the centre of what I was trying to do in the drama – both for myself and for helping 2F to enter the world of *Smith*. One key feature of the book is the interplay of trust and betrayal among Smith's acquaintances, with the ever-present threat of violent death at the hands of the executioner or of each other.

I was intrigued to know how it would go – and pretty nervous about it. Maggie didn't help when, learning what I was going to try, she invited herself along to watch: 'I'm free then. I'd like to see it. You don't mind, do you?' Before I could stop myself I'd said 'No. . . .'

'Right, fine, see you tomorrow then,' and she breezed off.

Hell! it's bad enough taking a risk you're not sure you can cope with. But having someone with Maggie's experience to come in and watch you – oh hell!

After this third lesson Maggie and I had time for a proper talk – which in the event I found very helpful. It went something like this:

Maggie: How are you feeling about it?

Me: Well, I'm annoyed with myself – very annoyed. The session got off to a good start and then somehow I lost it. I just wasn't good at handling it later on.

Maggie: I certainly agree about your good start. The class are obviously 'into' this work – I thought they worked quite crisply and purposefully on the still images.

Me: Yes, and I was pleased at the way they went back into the tavern – I get the feeling they feel comfortable there. And I was delighted at the way they responded to my brief bit of role-work. You could feel the attention and the tension as a quite tangible thing – when I looked round at them all it was, 'Oh, he won't pick on me will he?' I was very surprised (and relieved) at how that whole bit worked so well.

Maggie: Yes, you'd got a strong, clear tension in the drama, informed by that real tension of 'who will teacher choose?' And David was very strong when you accused him, wasn't he? He chose an interesting defence didn't he? 'Yes, I shopped him, but only because the runners were chasing him and he was making for the Red Lion. I shopped him to save myself and the rest of you.' You'd chosen the right person there. What about the girl who volunteered to take over your role?

Me: Kathy, yes. . . .

Maggie: Did you expect her to be so strong?

Me: No, not at all, I was amazed when she volunteered and was so keen to do it. I was doubtful that she'd cope at all well. So again I was delighted. . . . It's something that's striking me more and more about this drama business – even though I've not done a lot, I've seen quite a lot of evidence of kids like Kathy suddenly contributing, offering themselves in a way they don't in more conventional class discussions. It's as if changing the conventions and the rules of interaction, and letting them take a role (rather than being themselves) is amazingly releasing – it sort of takes the pressure off. Yet in a funny way, in a different way, there's more pressure on – there was Kathy telling the whole group about this betrayal, believing in it strongly and *knowing the class drama depended on her and coping marvellously with that knowledge.*

Maggie: It was interesting the way she began playing your role by repeating nearly exactly your words and gestures, then suddenly took off by herself.

Me: Yes, and once Kathy and David got going they didn't need me at all. Well not in a pivotal role, but they and the class needed support still – they needed a helping hand of some kind to find their direction, and I didn't manage to give that to them. At first things just moved by themselves, and Kathy's and David's examples pulled in the rest of the class. A lot (though not all) of them spoke seriously and to the point in role. But then gradually they ran out of steam, and the arguments started to go round in circles. I felt I wanted to try and help move things on from within the drama, if possible, but well. . . .

Maggie: Yes, I found it interesting to watch what you did once you had lost your initial role. You operated very much as teacher rather than as somebody in the tavern. For a start, when you got the class to move into the circle to discuss Kathy's accusation and

David's defence, you allowed yourself to be left physically outside that circle. That in itself might not have been a problem – except it represented the fact that you were using outside (teacherly) ways of thinking and operating, rather than inside (role) ones. Look at the way you moved them into that circle. Your instinct to change the spacing was right, I'm sure. The intensity of the occasion, if it was to be sustained, meant you needed to get them away from their tables in the tavern – they were too dispersed. But how did you do it? You, as teacher, stopped the drama and asked them to get into a circle. So you set up a 'discussion', not a dramatic experience. It needed bunching, a crowd – not a formal debating circle – and you could have got it much more efficiently (and achieved greater intensity) if in role as one of them – no need to define it any more – you'd said, 'I want to take a good look at this traitor', and moved towards the accused man, while signalling strongly, 'Come on', to the rest with your head or your arm. Then you'd have got a crowd pressing round David, with that feeling of: 'We're going to get the truth from you.'

Me: Yes, I could feel myself being squeezed out of the drama – not knowing how to get back in. In a way I was afraid that if I did go back in, they would then sit back and expect me to 'run the show'.

Maggie: Whether that happens depends on what you say and do, on how you operate in the role. For example, you were obviously concerned to spread the range of contributions so that everybody had their say. I presume that was why at one point you stopped the drama and asked them, with the hand-on-shoulder routine, to speak aloud what their role felt about the accusation – whether it was true or not, and what they could do about the situation.

Me: Yes, that was it.

Maggie: Wouldn't it have been possible to make brief interjections *in role* which pulled more people in? Such as:

'Toby kept himself to himself. I don't really know him – I've no idea whether he'll shop us or not. *You've* worked with him sometimes – what do you think?' or

'Jack's been accused of shopping Toby. (*To a member of Jack's footpad gang.*) Where were you when all this was happening?' or

'You know Nell (*role-name of Jack's accuser*). Is she telling the truth? Is there any reason she might be lying?' or

'You're keeping very quiet. Do you know something we don't?'

All of these could have pulled folk into the exchange *in role* – could have demanded that they make a highly specific contribution to the scene. In fact what you asked them to speak about, with the hand-on-shoulder business, was just too general, so you didn't get a lot that way. After the first few, most of them repeated what previous folk had said. And it was 'cool' not 'hot'. Thieves, pickpockets and footpads don't coolly debate whether somebody has betrayed them and what to do with him. They get worked up about it. You tended to keep trying to move it towards rational discourse – towards the kind of discussion that might happen in an English lesson.

Me: Yes, yes, I know exactly what you mean. When towards the end I got them to vote on what to do with Jack, and the majority said, 'Let him off', it felt like a vote at the end of a class debate. In fact it wasn't a vote on what to do with Jack, it was really a popularity poll for David. By that stage they'd really slid out of role completely.

Maggie: I wonder how the people in the Red Lion would have 'voted'? Not hands up in a circle and count, that's for sure. Supposing, for example, you'd got them one by one to go and stand by Nell, if like her they wanted him killed; or by Jack if they were satisfied with his explanation. That would have put each of them clearly on the spot – and would have built the tension steadily. And you might have begun the vote by placing a 'dagger' (the execution instrument) on a table between Jack and Nell, so that the choice was clear and stark.

Me: I suppose it all boils down to two things: thinking more *within* the drama. . . .

Maggie: Yes, thinking in 'now' time, not 'then' time – and helping the kids to make it happen in 'now' time.

Me: Yes, and the other thing is trying to think quickly, to find the right direction for the drama. It's difficult when you haven't got a definite plan to work to.

Maggie: Well, yes it can be to start with. But it gets easier. And you need to remember that the kids can help you with determining the direction and shaping of the work. When you have a class who've become as committed as these were it's daft to try and decide it all yourself. You've managed to get to the point where you're willing to try dropping a pebble into a pool and seeing what ripples result. You let them have their head *within* the drama to some extent. What about getting them to make decisions *about* the drama – you know, you can stop the drama and say: 'I can see two or three directions this drama could go in.' (And you list and explain them.) 'Which direction do you want it to go?' That's not moving away from 'now' time – it's asking them what kind of experience they want to have when they are in 'now' time.

Me: It's not easy, this drama business is it?

Maggie: No it's not easy, but nothing worthwhile is. You're on the way now. What are you going to do next?

10

JOURNAL FIVE:
BEOWULF

Teacher role

- confrontation role, used to provoke 'resistance' in role
- teacher supports them out of role ('gives permission') to resist him in role

Language possibilities

- shift in teacher–pupil (and pupil–pupil) relationship within the drama creates new contexts, new relationships in which new language can develop
- teacher in role as model for new language required

When and why to stop the drama

Finding a direction within the drama

I had to cover a class for Maggie the other day – she'd gone down with flu. It was a double period with 2J. There was no work set, so I asked them what work they were doing currently; they had nearly finished *Dragon Slayer*, they said. On the spur of the moment an idea came to me and I decided to act on it: 'I think we'll do some drama', I told the class. 2J would be well accustomed to drama, having Maggie as their teacher. I thought I could try an experiment – after all it would have no consequences if it misfired, I was only with them for seventy minutes!

I'd recently been looking through a drama handbook, *Drama Structures* by O'Neill and Lambert, which is generally quite a useful book, and, among other things, I'd come across an outline of some work on the legend of Beowulf. I used it as the basis for what I did with 2J. Briefly the outline starts like this:

1 Class sitting on a circle of chairs. Teacher tells class they are to be Beowulf's followers (they are currently reading the legend) and sorts out with them how they would enter the hall when Beowulf had summoned them.

2 Teacher in role as Beowulf greets each pupil in turn with a 'special handshake' and asks him/her to say the oath with him. (Class have previously decided it is 'All for one and one for all'.) Then all repeat oath in unison.

3 Beowulf tells his companions of Grendel's depredations on Hrothgar's people. He wishes to help Hrothgar and knows many of them will wish to accompany him, 'but first of all he would like to present them with a challenge. Will they be prepared to undertake some tests which he has devised? He needs to be reminded once again of his companions' great skills. The tests are designed to illustrate those qualities which may be essential if the venture is to be a success.' (O'Neill and Lambert, 1982, 207).

4 Test of stealth is played – an adapted version of the game 'Keeper of the Keys'. At intervals during this Beowulf asks his companions if they can recall times when this kind of stealth was essential to them.

Further tests and talk preparatory to the expedition follow.

This was designed as a careful, 'safe' plan. But I borrowed

and altered it to test myself in a teacher-role with a much greater element of risk:

1 I intended to let the class have a large hand in shaping the drama. For example once (or if) the commitment to go on the expedition was made, instead of having a predetermined set of 'tests' and preparation I would say, 'My companions, advise me, how best shall we prepare for this adventure? How shall we make ourselves ready in body and spirit?' I thought that it was important that we attend to the mental/spiritual preparation as well as the physical. But the manner of our preparations was to be decided by the whole group debating in role.

2 I intended to behave in role in a manner that might raise doubts in Beowulf's followers about the wisdom of the enterprise proposed: to set a bait and see how or whether they took it.

I started with the ritual greeting and oath-taking much as outlined in *Drama Structures*, taking care to establish strong eye-contact with each person for the greeting and oath-taking – this eye-contact I now know is a key to communicating and assessing seriousness. 2J immediately matched my seriousness with theirs – they weren't going to waste time. I could sense them gearing themselves up for the drama. I guess that's the result of Maggie's work with them. Unlike the plan above, I chose the words of the oath: 'I swear to serve my people and Beowulf, their leader, while there is breath in my body'. This made it more explicitly an oath of allegiance, or obedience – in fact of *dual* allegiance and obedience, which was important for what followed.

Another key change in the plan was that in role I pressed the whole class to make a commitment to the expedition, immediately after outlining Hrothgar's problem with Grendel. I spoke, roughly as follows:

My friends, I have great news for you. Great news. Long hours I sat here in my hall, fondly recalling memories of our past adventures. Too long have I sat, living on such memories – for many years have gone by since we last put on our war gear and accomplished heroic deeds. Of late I have longed to take up the sword again, to recapture the glory I know of old. We have all grown soft in these soft, peaceful days where little is left to do but eat and drink and tell stories.

Now, now, my friends, my subjects, here at last is an adventure for us – a chance to show what Beowulf's people are made of.

(*There followed an outline of Grendel's predations on Hrothgar's people.*)

We must prepare ourselves for journey and for battle forthwith. We set sail for glory in three days. Now, before we begin our preparations, I ask you all to repeat your oath of allegiance to me and to swear that you will follow me loyally in this adventure.

Rapidly I summoned the pupil nearest to my right hand to kneel before me and re-take the oath (now significantly changed both in its content and manner of taking): 'I swear to serve you, Beowulf, and to follow you against Grendel, while there is breath in my body'.

I had made the expedition and the oath an *issue* they could take up, if they wished. There was much to disturb in Beowulf's appeal to his followers. Would they respond to these 'invitations to question or deny' I had given them? Or would they accept the call to battle? I rushed the first couple of pupils into taking the oath, meanwhile trying to sense what the reaction of the class was. Maybe I needed to stop the drama and say, 'How do you feel about what Beowulf has said to you?' Maybe, because they didn't know me, they weren't sure whether in role they could question, challenge or oppose this teacher? We could sort that out explicitly in discussion: 'So are you going to take the oath, or . . . ?'

I didn't stop it, because something was obviously stirring: a couple of boys about a third of the way round the circle were conferring quietly but urgently. Press on, and see what happens!

The first eight or nine took the oath, though some appeared uncertain or quietly reluctant. I ignored this and simply pushed on. Now I had reached the two boys.

'Now it is your turn to take the oath. Step forward and kneel before me!' I said to the first of them in ringing, challenging tones. He didn't move. There was a pause. The whole class knew something was about to happen. He looked briefly at his companion, who nodded.

'I won't take this oath, Beowulf.'

'Nor will I', his companion said.

'Come, come. This is no time for joking. We have urgent business in hand. We sail in three days.'

'We're not joking, Beowulf', said the first boy. 'We won't go with you to fight Grendel. Not unless you give us some better reasons to go.'

I stopped the drama very briefly, just to say to the two boys, 'I think what you have just said would make Beowulf very bewildered and very angry. Are you ready for that to happen? You'll need to be strong-minded to stand up to him – he's been a leader all his life and is used to obedience. Can you manage?' (I felt I needed to say this, so that it was clear that standing up to Beowulf, though it might be difficult, was permitted.) They said they could cope, and we went straight back into the role.

I accused them of cowardice, of treachery, of oath-breaking. They stood up to all this courageously and firmly, asserting that I was trying to drag them all off on a long and dangerous expedition for my own personal glory, without thinking of the consequences; that many of them were old now and unused to fighting – such an army was bound to meet disaster. Angrily I turned away from them to the rest of the class who had not yet been asked to take the oath, saying I would receive their allegiance first, then we would come back to these two oath-breakers to determine how they should be punished.

Briefly, I stopped the drama again to say, 'I don't know how the rest of Beowulf's companions are thinking and feeling. It's up to you whether you take the oath, or side with the two rebels, or take another position entirely. Let's see what happens, shall we?'

Stepping back into role, I repeated my words about returning later to the two oath-breakers. A girl spoke.

'Beowulf, give us more time to consider this matter. We don't – we don't know what this adventure involves. We should think and talk about it – then we can reach the best decision about whether we can help Hrothgar and his people. You are rushing us all.'

My angry reaction brought in others who argued variously that:

– we owed nothing to Hrothgar – let him fight his own battles;
– we should go, if help was needed, but with more time to plan, and to make provision for our absence;
– it was difficult to leave our families and farms for an indefinite period;
– they should have confirmation from Hrothgar himself of the problem and the need for help before rushing off;
– we should go if Hrothgar paid us well;
– Beowulf should ask younger men to go;
– Beowulf was 'trying to bully us into doing what he wanted, without considering us'.

Through this section, though glowering, I spoke little because they were feeding each other, and I wanted to give space for them to do that, but to this last comment, I asserted vehemently that I was their leader, they owed me obedience and they had only just taken an oath to serve me – how could they refuse, or debate whether, to repeat the oath?

'Beowulf. It is *not* the same oath!' A girl spoke heatedly. 'We all swore to serve our people and you as our leader. But this second oath says nothing about our people – only about serving you and going to war.'

'Yes', a boy followed, 'we've always served you before

because you did your best for all of us. But now you seem to be out just for your own glory and you don't think about us.'

I stormed away from the group, shouting that they were my subjects, owed me allegiance, and I would give them a short while to recover from the madness that was infecting them. Then I would come back and accept their allegiance generously, forgetting all that had just passed. I sensed that I needed to get away from the group, that they needed time to talk among themselves in role about what was to be done: that the strength they were acquiring would grow more rapidly with Beowulf 'away' for a bit.

They bunched and spoke quietly (though urgently) to each other, so that I would hear little of what was going on – a problem for me, as I wanted to 'tune in' to what was going on, in order to plan my next move. But they obviously felt the need for 'secrecy'. Odd phrases were audible to my straining ears:

– 'send messengers to Hrothgar';
– 'too old to be our leader';
– 'living in the past'.

After three or four minutes, they turned towards me and one of them said, 'Sir, can you not come back as Beowulf, until we're ready?'

'OK. Why don't you send someone for me when you're ready?'

The class were really taking charge now! The huddle grew tighter. The voices quieter. Another five or six minutes passed before one of them came to fetch me. The rest stood in a block facing me, a small group in front, including the two boys who had started the challenge to Beowulf's authority. The girl who had earlier commented on the way I changed the oath, spoke for them all:

'Beowulf, we have all agreed. None of us will go with you on this adventure. It's too rushed and not well thought out . . .'

'I am your leader. I command you!'

'Beowulf!' she continued firmly, 'You are old. We must have a new leader.'

I reacted angrily, accusing the two boys of setting this rebellion up deliberately to usurp my authority, and then insisted that some of them had already taken the second oath – they were bound to follow me, whatever the rest said. We could deal with Grendel without them; we were not afraid. They dealt firmly but patiently with all this – they knew they had won and there was no point in being angry.

Finally, I said, 'So this is how you repay me for the long years I led you, looked after you all and brought fame and wealth to all of you. This is your gratitude.' I spoke quietly, as if hurt deeply. There was a pause. Then the same girl who had announced their decision moved towards me:

'Beowulf, we *are* grateful. We shan't forget what you've done. We will always remember those times. But things are different now. You are old. I am old. We are not as strong as we used to be. We don't always think so clearly as we once did. Let's enjoy our old age. Let it be quiet and peaceful.'

I looked at her, at the rest, at her again, without speaking, then walked slowly away, shoulders bowed. There wasn't far to walk in that classroom, so when I reached the wall I 'froze' because I wanted to hold the feeling that was there in the room for a little longer.

Then, grinning broadly, I walked back, asked them to sit down, thanked them (I meant it!) for making such a fascinating drama with me.

'At the end there, I felt I knew just how Beowulf would feel in those circumstances: defeated; quite unable to understand; his whole world destroyed really. How did *you* feel as you watched him walk away?'

'It was sad,' a boy replied, 'but there was nothing else we could do.'

'I wished I could help him to understand', said the girl who had spoken last to Beowulf. 'But I wasn't sure how – whether he'd ever listen.'

In the few minutes remaining of the lesson we talked briefly about ways Beowulf's people, and their new leader, whoever he might be, could help Beowulf to understand and to feel that he was still valued and respected though not able to be what he once was. We also began to discuss how people generally found it difficult to adapt to changed circumstances in their lives. Various examples came up.

Growing old
Losing your job
Your children growing up and not being children any more.
Refugees
Parents separating or dying

It took me a while to come down from the 'high' this lesson generated. When I did and looked back reasonably coolly at it, this session pointed up all sorts of things for me:

1 *The way drama work can become self-generating*. Out of the drama had come this notion of 'adapting to changed circumstances' and the class were offering examples of this, any of which could have given us a context for the next drama.

2 *How drama can affect the language children use in the classroom*. Throughout this session I could sense all the children working to find the right words for the situation, knowing that everyday language wasn't quite it, that something else was needed. I need to look at the possibilities here a whole lot more.

3 *How, by the adoption of role, in an 'as if' situation, teacher and children can interact with, and relate to, each other in a totally different way than that of teacher and learner* (indeed in so many different ways). In this Beowulf session look at the way the power in the drama (and the responsibility for it) changed hands. I suspect that this shift in relationship, away from the customary pattern of classroom communication and authority has a lot to do with the language possibilities that drama offers, and this session has revealed to me very

clearly how this shift can 'release' pupils and help them shape their own work and learning. The possibilities, the implications are endless. Wow!

4 *More specifically I think I've learnt something about finding a direction in drama work and about when to stop the drama.* This class changed the direction of the drama from being about 'preparing for a military expedition', to 'whether we should go on it', and then to 'Beowulf is no longer fit to lead'. These shifts were accomplished 'on their feet', within the drama. With a less experienced and confident group (i.e. any of *my* classes!) I probably would have had to stop the drama much more often:

   a) to clarify the direction. For example, 'This drama seems to be changing: it's becoming about whether Beowulf can remain our leader, rather than just whether we go to hunt Grendel or not. Is that the direction we want it to take?'

   b) to give the class the opportunity to think things through and consider the implications of a scene before we do it, for example just what would going to hunt Grendel mean to these people: what disruption to their lives and work; what arrangements would they have to make (for harvests, etc.); what prospect of reward would it hold out? And bearing all this in mind, how might we respond when Beowulf tells us we are to leave on an expedition in three days' time?

   c) to remind them of the need for seriousness

   d) to sort out more explicitly how things are to be done, for example how to use space and distance to create appropriate feeling and tension. This group just seemed to know how to place themselves when they called Beowulf back. Other groups might well have needed me to say, 'How are you going to position yourselves so that Beowulf sees that you are all together and strong in your decision?'

e) for all sorts of reasons, but not merely if the drama is stumbling and needs remedial action. I can see now it is often important to stop it when it's going well.

11
DRAMA AND LANGUAGE

NEW CONTEXT CREATED

NEW ROLES ESTABLISHED

NEW RELATIONSHIP IN OPERATION

NEW LANGUAGE DEMANDS MADE

LANGUAGE DEMANDS TACKLED

LANGUAGE DEVELOPMENT

(from Wilson and Cockcroft, p. 19)

Figure 11

I think Figure 11 offers a good start into understanding how drama can promote language development.

Drama is a powerful tool for developing language because when we step into a drama we agree to suspend our 'real' context, the classroom, and the set of 'real' roles and relationships which go with that context. *New* contexts, *new* roles and *new* relationships begin to operate, because we agree to operate in an 'as if' or fictional world. Those new contexts, roles and relationships can make very different language demands on us from those of the 'real' classroom, so new possibilities for language use and development are opened up.

Language development in a new context

It is the shift to 'as if' that is crucial. Angela Wilson and Roy Cockcroft offer a brief but fascinating transcript from a drama lesson (part of which is reproduced on pp. 118–19) to amplify their diagram. Here I will only quote their summary of the language demands made on the children as evidence of the depth of language challenge the move into 'as if' can make:

> How do you talk to a Prince who knows a lot less than you do about war, whom you suspect to be a coward, but who has the power to do anything he wishes? How do you advise him to do what you think is the best policy when you expect that his cowardice will not allow him to take that advice? How do you encourage him without being patronising? How do you discuss military matters with a man who shares none of the language of warfare?   (p. 19)

One interesting thing about this example is that the Prince was, in the 'real' context of the classroom, the children's teacher. *One of the important features of the shift to an 'as if' context is that it has the potential to change quite significantly the patterns of communication and interaction in a classroom, and the teacher's part in those patterns:*

> Educational researchers have been aware for some time that the focal role of the teacher as the constant source of authority in classrooms leads pupils to become cut off from their own self-motivated desire to learn. Pupils tend to enter the instructional world of the teacher by accepting the frame of reference that is provided for them. This establishes a dependency relationship that works against the independent behaviour the teacher is attempting to establish.
>
> (Carroll, 1983, 9)

Language development through new role-relationships

One of the opportunities offered by taking on roles in an 'as if' situation is that there can be significant shifts in role-relationship between teacher and pupil, and in particular where the power and responsibility lies in that role-relationship. Consider the following brief extract from Wilson and Cockcroft's transcript of pupils (in role as military advisers) with their teacher (the Prince). The advisers (three girls) have just explained their proposed defence plan, when the Prince confesses to them his personal difficulties about the forthcoming battle:

Prince: I think I am a coward. (Silence)
I don't think I could go through with it. Just to see all those men charging at me.

Adviser 1: Well, you could command the battle.

Adviser 2: Where they (the enemy) are they're camping in a field. We're on higher ground so we'd have more chance of charging at them.

Adviser 3: And we said we were going to surprise them.

Adviser 1: They'd have to go up the hill. They'd have to sort of run up the hill and if there's stockades they're

	going to have to climb over those or go round them and it will take a lot longer.
Prince:	I'll tell you what. I'll agree to fight if I can be protected.
Adviser 1:	We could have a couple, a few of our warriors sort of guarding you, a bodyguard so that you wouldn't get hurt.
Prince:	I wouldn't have to go out in front like your King does, would I?
Adviser 2:	Well, depending on whether you wanted to. We can't say you go in front.
Adviser 1:	We can't say, look, you've got to go in front.
Prince:	You can if you think it's best. I'm handing the whole thing over to you.

(Wilson and Cockcroft, 17–18)

Then the children try to find ways in which the Prince can lead, and participate 'honourably' in the battle, while being protected from danger and from his own thresholds of fear. Although in terms of formal authority, the Prince is the 'boss', the actual dynamic of the situation is very different. The weight of responsibility rests with the advisers (the children) and their Prince (the teacher) is dependent on them not only for military advice but for support in knowing how to cope with a leadership role for which he feels himself unfit.

Journal 5 offers another interesting example of a teacher taking a leadership role, yet actually handing power to the class. In this case it is because in the drama he signals to the class through his role, 'I am trying to take more power over you than I deserve or you can afford to give. You need to resist me in spite of all the old ties of friendship and loyalty.' At a key point the teacher (as teacher) gives specific 'permission' for the class to resist his role within the drama – by making clear the distinction between himself as teacher, and, in the drama, as Beowulf. He asks if they are 'ready' for Beowulf to react angrily: 'You'll need to be strong to stand up to him – he's been

a leader all his life and is used to obedience. Can you manage?'
Often it is very important to signal clearly that teacher behaviour *in role* (especially anger) is quite separate from teacher
behaviour, and that the class has 'permission' to respond
differently – in this case, 'permission' to resist and win.

It seems to me that two key (and related) conditions need
to be met to overcome the problem of teacher control of
communication and pupil dependency:

1 A shift in power, as between 'teacher' and 'taught'.
2 A shift so that the problem or task becomes important to
   pupils and teacher *in and of itself* – the problem is not merely
   set for the pupils by the teacher. Rather, it is beyond them
   both, and they must both work at, or struggle with, it.

I have a real sense in the transcript above that the problem,
'Can the advisers help the Prince to play his part in saving his
country from attack, and if so, how can they best do that?' is a
problem that pupils and teacher confront as equals. I think this
illustrates nicely the relationship between the two shifts: it is
when the learning task, the dilemma within the drama,
assumes an intrinsic importance of its own – when it *matters* –
that the shift in power between teacher and pupils can occur,
because the problem is bigger than them both. (I want to stress
that I am *not* trying to say that it is *only through drama* that
these shifts can occur – only that drama is *one economical and
effective way of achieving them*, with the particular advantage
that it temporarily suspends the 'real' network of relationships
in a classroom, and replaces them with another fictional network which has a logic of its own, not dependent on the 'real'
network.

I will also argue that, through the same process, *real shifts
can occur in relationships between pupils*: that drama can
enable them to step beyond their normal patterns of interaction, and make new demands of relationship and language on
each other. I do so with some caution, however. I am not
wanting to deny that in a drama 'the real social network

underlies and informs the nature and quality of their involvement' (McGregor *et al.*, 1977, 18). Nor that 'Sometimes the real tensions are so urgent that they prevent the symbolic level from functioning' (McGregor *et al.*, 1977, 68).

Clearly if there is a marked lack of congruence between the way pupils see themselves and the roles they are asked to take on, or if the feeling demanded of the work makes them feel 'exposed', then it is likely that they will reject the drama, either actively or passively. This means the teacher *must* take account of the 'real social network' in his or her planning and teaching. It does not mean that s/he cannot hope to get pupils to move beyond that 'real' network within the drama, to a greater or lesser extent.

The transcript which follows is a clear example of how the demands of role in a fictional context can create a significant shift in relationships. The children, a second year group, were in role as villagers, in a meeting they had called themselves early one Saturday morning to discuss as a matter of urgency the Ministry of Agriculture's decision to gas a nearby badger set after a complaint by a farmer whose cattle were affected by bovine tuberculosis.

Steven (Vicar):	Hello, thanks for coming, you know I think the problem we are all worried over – Neil would like to say something.
Neil:	As the vicar says, there's going to be problems down at the badgers' set, they're going to start gassing them. I'd like to know what you think about this. I think it's wrong.
Courteney:	Well, I've just been down the council – and they were shut. I've got this letter – I had permission to start building – it's my job – and now I can't 'cos they're gassing. I don't know when they'll be finished – but now I'm not working, not

	earning – and who'll want to buy houses where badgers have been gassed – now I'll have to look for another site – It's – it's not right.
Steven P.:	I think it's dangerous for other wildlife round here, and what if it gets into the water?
Neil:	Are you against it then?
Steven P.:	Yeah.
Mark (Village Policeman):	But you can't do anything – I mean to stop it.
Paula:	Can't we buy some land and move the badgers?
Neil:	But it's happening now!
Scott (Owner of Pub):	I go down that set every week, every week for years, it's not right. That's all I got to say.
	(to PC) Why didn't you tell me?
Neil:	(to PC) What do you know about this?
Mark (PC):	I got instructions to go down there and keep people away – that's all I have been told.
Neil:	Does anyone here agree with this gassing?

There then follows a heated exchange between those most opposed to the gassing of the badgers, and the farmer (the teacher) whose cattle are affected. This ends when the farmer leaves saying:

	I'm sorry you feel like this, but I want to save my cows and my farm. I can't afford to stand here all morning arguing.
	(Exit from drama.)
Gary:	Those badgers have got a right to live –
Scott:	Thousands of people have seen them,

	they even made a film of them for the telly.
Heidi:	They make our village famous.
Neil:	So what are we going to do?
Gary:	I think we should stop them.
	(*Indecipherable hubbub.*)
Neil:	What about everyone else in this hall? What do the rest of you think? Maybe we could get down there and stop them somehow.
Dione:	I'm going to take my kids to my sister's for the weekend.
Nadine:	Yes, me too – I don't want any trouble or danger.
	(*Indecipherable hubbub . . . arguments about being involved or not.*)
Gary:	(*shouting*) We'll need wire and sticks.
Neil:	Quiet everybody, c'mon, calm, look . . . QUIET! Who here is in favour of the gassing (*two hands are raised*). Right then, who's against? (*Multitude of hands raised.*) Now, who wants to get down there and stop it? (*About two-thirds raise their hands.*)
Courteney:	How we going to stop them, that's what I want to know.
Gary:	We'll stop them, don't worry about that.
Richard:	We'll smash the barriers and sit on the badgers' holes before they put gas in.
	(*Excited hubbub/babble, difficult to distinguish anything clearly.*)
Mark (PC):	You can't do that.
Gary:	You try stopping us.
Mark (PC):	Think – you can't just charge off and sit down and smash equipment. It's against

	the law for a start – I'll have to stop you. (*Mutterings from the group.*)
	No, quiet, I mean I've been told, ent I, I've got to keep people away.
Neil:	Well, do you think it's right to kill the badgers?
Scott:	You always come down the set with me – you don't want to help kill them do you?
Mark:	But it's my job to keep the law.
Scott:	Whose side are you on?
Mark:	It's my job.
Gary:	Stuff your job – you want to save the badgers don't you?
Mark:	Look – I have to keep order. If you break the law, I'll have to arrest you – I mean, I know you, but y'know, it's my job.
Neil:	Well, we're going to stop them! Who agrees?
	(*Chorus of agreement.*)
	Right then, let's go.

At this point the teacher stops the drama. There are five minutes of the lesson left and there needs to be time to reflect on the implications of this meeting.[1]

I want to draw your attention particularly to the contributions of Neil, Scott and Mark. Neil is not normally a leader within the class, yet he has been placed as a leader in the village community and functions as such: he works hard to elicit others' views, and to find a suitable way in which the feelings expressed can be channelled into appropriate action. He is largely responsible for the overall direction and conduct of the meeting. He has his own views, as other (omitted) parts of the transcript make very clear, but above all he tries to help the village community as a whole find its voice and make its decision.

Scott, earlier in the drama, had established for himself two crucial features of his role, which shape his behaviour and language in the exchange transcribed: first, a keen interest in wildlife, and, secondly, a strong friendship with the village policeman. We see him reassessing his friendship when the two factors come into conflict.

The village policeman is played by Mark, whose contribution is particularly interesting. He is quite a dominant character within the class, but not verbally articulate – he is a physical lad. In this transcript we see him *reaching for the right words* to cope with the conflict between his duty as a policeman on the one hand, and his personal preferences, the anger of his particular friend, Scott, and quite widespread antipathy from the villagers on the other. It was an exceptional experience for Mark to find most of his classmates solidly and articulately opposed to him. This was made possible by the move to an 'as if' situation.

The 'reality' of the drama

So, my argument is that *drama, because it suspends or modifies the 'real' context and social network of the classroom, in favour of an 'as if' context and network, can provide an enormous variety of opportunities for different kinds of language demand and development.* (See Figure 11, p. 116.)

Because in drama we operate in an 'as if' world, the choice of contexts for language use is literally limitless. One can create a drama situation to provoke any kind of language demand – spoken or written – a teacher might wish to make. However, a real danger lurks in the view of drama as providing 'contexts for language use'. Often this view is taken to mean that, as teachers, we provide lots of varied contexts in which children can 'practise their language skills'. There are two words I take exception to in this phrase: the first is 'practise', the second is 'skills'.

Our use of language is challenged when *real demands*

are made on it – not when we are asked to 'practise' skills against the time we might need them for real. What Robert Protherough says of learning to write seems to me to be true of all language development work:

> [it] depends upon seeing the *point* of that activity, on extending the range of *real purposes* for which it is used, on having available appropriate models and demonstrations of writing, and on a supporting environment that provides encouragement and appropriate audiences. (1983, 16. My emphasis.)

Now I have emphasized that drama is *not real* – that it operates by creating an 'as if' or fictional world. But what is important, for my present purposes, is that, as human beings, we have a marked propensity to become absorbed in an 'as if' world, so that it begins to *feel real*: not real in the sense that it is actually happening, but real in the sense that the problems faced and the outcomes *matter* to the participant (or, in a piece of theatre, to the spectator). In the transcripts above it *mattered* to find a way of helping the Prince to cope with the problem; it *mattered* whether the badgers were gassed – and because these things mattered, the participants were challenged to find the language which met their purposes within the 'as if' context. Also important to note is that they were attending primarily not to the language itself (not exercising their language skills), but to the pressures and needs of the 'as if' situation in which they found themselves. Paradoxically I think it is broadly true to say (I want to qualify this somewhat later) that language development is likely to be most rich in drama work, when the attention of both pupils and teacher is primarily focused on the demands of the dramatic situation, rather than on the language being used. This is not to say that a teacher cannot have very specific language aims in drama work – only that having decided upon those aims, and found a drama form s/he believes will serve those aims, s/he must attend above all to getting the drama to work (through the use of appropriate tensions, symbols and signs, etc.), so that it begins to *matter* to the pupils. The most elegant plan for language development through drama will not succeed if the children do not care enough about the problem in the drama to try and meet the challenges (including the language challenge) it offers.

Concreteness and abstraction

Another paradox about drama in the service of language development is that its strength resides both in its *concreteness* and in its *power to encourage abstraction*. I want to look at both in turn: first, its concreteness.

Drama is nothing if not concrete. Its material, as Suzanne Langer said, is the 'immediate, visible responses of human beings' (1953, 306). Margaret Donaldson (1978, 36) stresses the importance of creating learning situations which 'make human sense', that is, are embedded in a context of human purposes and interactions, and, particularly relevant to our purposes here, she argues, following John Mcnamara,

> that children are able to learn language precisely because they possess certain other skills – and specifically because they have a relatively well-developed capacity for making sense of certain types of situation involving direct and immediate human interaction. (1978, 36)

I was arguing in a similar vein earlier (see p. 79) when I said: 'Young people are, generally speaking, stronger at reading action, or words embedded-in-action, than they are at reading words alone. Drama allows them to explore these strengths in a highly focused way'. It is because our pupils have the capacity, and desire, to *make sense* of immediate, direct human interactions that drama is a valuable provoker of their language development – they constantly create new language demands on themselves through their attempts to make sense of the situations they find themselves in.

Although drama is 'the most concrete, least abstracted of the arts', and that, as I have tried to argue, is part of its strength (see p. 77); it is still an abstracting process. It is lifelike, yet it is a selection, a shaping, from life, and not life itself. It has the immediacy of life-events, yet because we are selecting and shaping we are distanced from it: we become absorbed in drama, we submit to the experience of it ('participant mode'), but we are also detached from it, aware of it, because we make, control and observe it ('spectator mode'). Both modes are present in any drama, though the balance will vary from drama to drama, and from moment to moment within a particular drama.

It is the 'spectator mode' that encourages *abstraction* in drama, that breeds *a reflective awareness of what is being created in the drama, including the language being used.* As Mike Fleming says:

> If a pupil in drama assumes the role of a leader of an expedition, he will be prompted to use language by virtue of the role (he will need to make plans and decisions and give instructions) but he will also be conscious of the structure and development of the play. *The fact that he is involved in a pretend situation will make him more conscious of the language he is using.*   (1982, 161. My emphasis.)

As Fleming also points out, a reflective awareness of language operates in drama in three different ways:

1 'An ongoing reflective element which is part of the drama process' (1982, 160). When one is most thoroughly immersed in a role, one never ceases to be oneself or to be aware of making a drama, and so to be conscious of its elements (including language) and how appropriately they are functioning.

2 More *specific* opportunities for reflection and reflective talk may be built into a drama. This can be achieved by framing the pupils in a way which demands such reflection. More of this later; here I will offer only one example, from a drama

with a second year English class. They had been framed as members of the poor or criminal classes frequenting an eighteenth-century tavern. (Like Journal 4 the drama was linked to a reading of Garfield's *Smith*.) Two of their number were seized by the law in a raid on the tavern, after which a group of them, in the presence of the rest, murdered the tavern's landlady, who they felt sure had betrayed the two arrested. Later the landlady's ghost appeared to all of them, and the two were hanged. At the end of the drama, the class were asked by a historian (teacher in role) to look back on its events, still in role, from a time thirty years on: to recall the events and what they had meant to them then; how the events had changed their lives; and how they viewed them now.

3 Reflection on the drama occurs too when we step out of the drama to consider its progress and the implications of our actions within the 'as if' world. This happens at intervals during the development of a drama, and at the end of a piece of work. Often the discussion can move outside the specific context of the drama itself, as the key themes or underlying issues of the play are discussed. A clear example of this occurs at the end of the lesson described in Journal 5.

Sometimes in this reflection out of the drama, the *language* used in the drama will be looked at specifically. (It is here I want to qualify the statement I made a little earlier that 'language development is likely to be most rich in drama work, when the attention of both pupils and teacher is primarily focused on the demands of the dramatic situation, rather than on the language being used'.) Consider the following transcript, taken from a class discussion during a drama by 10- to 11-year-olds about the Old Testament story of Ahab, Jezebel and Elijah. Ahab, prompted by his foreign wife, Jezebel, intends to build a temple to Baal on the site of an existing village, which must therefore be levelled. Elijah, the prophet, acts as spokesman for the villagers. The children have been discussing any possible ways in which Ahab's plan might be thwarted – it is decided that the revelation that there is leprosy in the village might halt the King's plan. Once this, and a way of handling it within the next stage of the drama, have been decided, the teacher suggests they move back to the drama:

Teacher: Well, that's fine. Is there anything else anybody wants to talk about before we start again?

Pupil 1: Please, Sir, some people aren't treating me like a king, they are treating me like a peasant, they shout at me in any way.

Teacher: Ahab has a complaint that some people are still not treating him as a king, have you got anything to say about that, the rest of you?

Pupil 2: He doesn't treat us like peasants, he doesn't treat us like we are human people. If everyone raised their voices a bit to the king it would sound better and you wouldn't get so much noise like horses' shoes, like Mr Harrison suggested, there wouldn't be much of a crowd closing up in front of the king, the guards would keep them back. If the king sounded more royal and spoke this way, sometimes he trips up when he is speaking, well usually the king speaks slow so as not to make mistakes. The people shout too much to the king, they move up and shout too much, they don't treat him like a king.

Teacher: Well, Ahab, what would you do as a king if you were Ahab himself, and you are Ahab yourself, these people are moving up towards you and doing this kind of thing, what ideas have you got?

Pupil 1: The guards could send them back or whip them back. He just lets them come forward and he doesn't do anything, he just lets them stand and come up to him and shout.

Teacher: What would you suggest then Elijah?

Pupil 2: He could tell his guards to get them back or he could order them to be silent, tell them to get back himself.

Teacher: Any other ideas about that?

Pupil 2: He should have more power over the people. The way the people always come forward and people always seem to be on top of the king rather than the king being on top of the people. Sometimes when the king says 'Go back' they just keep on shouting at him and come forward.

Teacher: And do you think that people would really be like that?

Pupil 2: No because they know that they would probably get stoned to death or something.[2]

Here is a child of 10 or 11, in effect saying, 'Let's pay attention to our language in the drama we are doing. We need to get the language right for the drama to feel right.' His attention is more on the manner of their speaking than on its content, and the manner of speaking is seen as part of their overall behaviour (language embedded in action).

There are occasions and opportunities – which may simply arise, or can be aimed for and created by the teacher – when the language employed in the drama can be looked at explicitly. What is important is that, as in the transcript, the language is seen as part of the drama, and efforts to get the language right are seen not as a separate exercise, but as part of the effort to make the drama work. The language must feel right if the drama is to feel right. It would be very easy for this teacher to use the drama context he has established to get the children to pay very detailed attention to language. He might, for example, ask them to draw up a statement of appeal (spoken or written) by the villagers, against the royal edict condemning their homes to destruction. Because so much in the drama depends on the results of these statements, the children in role would be compelled by the logic of the drama to pay close attention (among other things) to:

Audience: What is likely to move, or fail to move, King Ahab?
Content: What arguments do we use?
Tone: Should we appeal through logic or feeling?
Vocabulary: What word(s) capture our meaning best here?
   (Many opportunities for weighing of alternatives.)
Style: Do we use the language of the king's proclamation or our
   own? Or something of both? Or . . . ?

*It is not difficult to construct a drama so that attention to
language is central to the work*. Indeed, as in Journal 1, pupils
can be framed so that attention to language is their central task.
There their purpose as museum staff (to discover what they
could about the historical period and meaning of the fragments
of writing) meant they had to pay close attention to the
content/narrative; to its patterning, watching for key, repeated
words, and motifs, and to connections and structure – was it
possible to sequence the material into a developing narrative
and to make inferences about gaps in the text from what was
given? It was, if you like, an extremely active 'active comprehension exercise'. There were ways available to press the class
even harder to attend to the language (task-pressure, not
teacher-pressure). Say by writing their own version of the gaps
in the narrative. Or by being confronted with additional
documentary material, which initial tests indicated to be of
similar age to the initial material, and reported to be found on
an adjacent site. Could they consider whether, on internal
textual evidence, the new material was (*a*) a further part of the
original saga; (*b*) a different author's telling of the same saga,
or a related one; or (*c*) a forgery, as other experts who had been
shown the material had reached very divided conclusions?

Varieties of language development

Thus far I have argued for drama as a tool for language
development and have tried to explain why that is so: how it
works to provoke new language challenges. Of course it is

difficult to prove such assertions. One can offer sample transcripts as evidence of the process one is trying to outline, and
they go some way to act as a testing ground for one's views and
theories.

I recently came across an Australian classroom research
project, which on the basis of quite extensive data, carefully
analysed, seems to offer clear evidence that drama offers a
significant range of educationally vital language opportunities,
which occur all too little in other kinds of work. The data was
collected in classrooms at the top end of primary schools, but
my guess is that the conclusions apply to both primary and
secondary schools. Those interested in the data should refer to
the report (Felton *et al.*, 1984). Here I shall merely summarize
some of the most significant findings.

1   *Drama provides opportunities for children to use language
for a wider variety of purposes than is general in classrooms.*
The general pattern in school classrooms seems to be that the
language used (whatever its form: reading, writing, talking, or
listening) is overwhelmingly *informational*. In the drama work
sampled, half the language used was informational, but the
other half was *expressive* or *interactional*.   These terms were
defined as follows:

> *Expressive* – the   speaker's   individual   expression   of
> thoughts, feelings and ideas – a personal view-
> point.
> *Interactional* – the focus of attention is on the person or
> persons being addressed as the speaker
> attempts to persuade, regulate behaviour,
> command, etc.
> *Informational* – the focus is neither on speaker nor audience,
> but on giving information.

2   The unusually high incidence of expressive and interactional language indicated that drama work:
a)   *Focuses attention on people, not merely things*, and so
redresses an important imbalance in the overall curriculum,

which tends to limit children's attention to 'facts' about the material world. Drama puts a human and social content back into eduction.

b) *Allows and encourages subjective responses and feelings to be expressed.* Children are able to bring both their feeling and their thinking to bear on the drama problem, and when they do their talk seems to be cognitively much richer.

3   *Expressive language, so prominent in drama, offers children greater opportunities for abstract thinking and more complex language use than informational language, which was the norm in most classroom activities.*

Informational language is predominantly	Expressive language is predominantly
concrete and generalized, rather than abstract	concerned with generalizations and abstractions (implications behind facts, rather than the facts themselves)
pitched in past and present tense	timeless in tense and employing the more complex syntactical structures associated with propositional modes of discourse
chronological	logical rather than chronological in sequence

Put another way, expressive language use needs to be encouraged if children are to be given the vital opportunities to speculate, imagine, predict, reason, and evaluate their own learning.

Table 11.1, on pages 136 and 137, is taken from the report and shows in some detail the contrast in language use between drama and many other kinds of classroom activity.

4   *Reflection times, during, and particularly at the end of a drama, are an especially rich time for language use.*
The research project's transcript analyses showed that *over half* the language used in reflection times was expressive in character. These are times when the class are invited to step back and consider from a distance what they have experienced

in the drama from the inside, to reflect on that experience and its implications. The emotional investment they have had in the drama encourages them to use language to articulate their thoughts and feelings about the experience, to try to make sense of it. Much of the talking is tentative, exploratory, with no sense of 'right' and 'wrong' answers – it is 'thinking aloud'.

The following comment from the report seems to me very significant:

> Reflective discussion after the drama was over was an established practice in very few of the classes involved in the project. However, after the early interviews with the children and the teacher – class interviews built into the project, *the value of such discussions became apparent to everyone concerned and the practice increased.* (p. 21: my emphasis)

The quality of the drama

To obtain quality of language in drama the teacher must attend to the quality of the drama. In particular, I think it is helpful to bear the following guidelines in mind.

1   WORK SLOW, WORK DEEP

Drama cannot be rushed. It needs time so that people can *grow into* the experience, grow into the role and viewpoint they are adopting, grow into the language they require for the 'as if' situation they find themselves in. As a general rule it is important to build slowly in order to establish belief and comfort in the role and the imagined context before creating strong tensions or high levels of intense feeling. What is important too is that the focus of the early activities is such as to build a foundation for the later challenges.

I once saw an infant teacher doing a drama related to a picture story book *The Happy Lion*. The drama challenge was essentially to be: Can we discover why the lion, who is our

Table 11.1

Language used in the school context (non-arts)	Question	Response	Level of Abstraction	Language used in classroom during drama
	What is happening?	Recording – what, when, where, who, how		
Most of the time	What happened?	Reporting – what, when, where, who how	Concrete	
	What happens?	Generalizing from specifics	Generalized	Most of the time *within* the imaginary context

Table 11.1 continued

Language used in the school context (non-arts)	Question	Response	Level of Abstraction	Language used in classroom during drama
Seldom	Why?	Speculating, predicting and theorizing	Abstract	All levels of abstraction occur
Hardly ever	What might happen if–?	Imagining	All levels used during reflection.	All the time (the imaginary context of drama)
	What does it matter – to you? to me? to others?	Evaluating		

Source: Felton *et al.*, 1984, p. 12.

friend and seemed so happy, has run away from the little zoo in our village? Can we help him and persuade him to come back? Now the teacher spent the greater part of the hour-long lesson working on establishing knowledge of, and belief in, the village. The children drew their houses or flats, placed them around the hall to represent the geographical layout of the village, went to the shops, etc. They were gaining a very clear sense of the *physical layout* of their 'as if' village, but what they really needed to know about was their *relationship with the lion before he ran away*. As a result, when the teacher in role as the zookeeper rushed into the village to tell everybody of the lion's escape, instead of the concern and involvement she hoped for, she found she was regarded by the children as a distraction from their current preoccupation with exploring and elaborating their village. What she had done was to put down foundations in a different place from where the house was to be built. They might have been good foundations for a play about 'They're going to drive a motorway through our village' but not for 'How can we help our friend, the lion?'

2   WHEN NECESSARY AND APPROPRIATE, BE ABLE TO FUNCTION IN ROLE WITHIN THE DRAMA

'Teacher in role' is sometimes favoured by some teachers, whereas others prefer, say, small group work. In fact *both* small group work and teacher-role are strategies that ought to be in the repertoire of *any* teacher using drama in the classroom. They each have different advantages and limitations, and are used at different times and for different purposes.

Teacher-role has certain specific advantages in terms of the quality of language used in a drama:

a) Teacher language (and behaviour/signalling) in role offers children a clear and concrete model to work from, in coping with the language shifts the drama demands. So the teacher must select his/her language and signalling with care!

(Journal 5 offers the clearest example of this, though several journal entries demonstrate it in one way or another.)

b) Being in role allows the teacher to put the pressure on, in terms of language demands, very directly and forcefully. Often the teacher in role will be able to make far greater or more precise demands on pupils' language capacities than pupils will make on themselves. (Journal 3 and Journal 5 both offer extensive examples of teacher-role being used – in very different ways! – to extend and challenge pupil language.)

3 BUILD OPPORTUNITIES FOR REFLECTION INTO THE DRAMA

Reflection – whether it be on the moral issues involved in a drama, on alternative outcomes, on ways of making the drama itself work better, or on the language used – will not occur naturally, by itself. It is not a spontaneous growth, but something that has to be consciously planned for and given space. This means

a) creating specific times for reflection out of role, and for in-role reflection of the kind mentioned earlier (see p. 128)

b) conducting all the drama work so that attention is focused not only on the action, but on the *meaning within the action*, not only on what people are doing, but upon what they are thinking and feeling, upon why they do what they do, and upon the possible consequences or implications of their actions. The way the teacher asks questions and they way s/he sets up drama tasks will to a large extent determine whether or not children's work in drama has a reflective dimension to it.

4 SELECT AN APPROPRIATE VIEWPOINT WITHIN THE TOPIC

Let us say that a class is working on a drama about the death of a young girl in a violent street incident which involved a large number of young people. There are many viewpoints the teacher might ask the class to adopt within the drama. They include:

a) the police seeking to discover what happened and who was responsible
b) the young people involved in the incident
c) a friend or relation trying to console the girl's family
d) a politician or social worker on a TV debate about young people and violence, speaking in the context of 'rising public anxiety' after this particular incident
e) the girl's parents looking back on their memories of their daughter.

The viewpoint selected is crucial. Each of these, though the topic is the same, will produce a different drama, with different learning areas and language opportunities. Even within each viewpoint there can be many shifts, or changes of gear. For example, within the basic viewpoint of the young people involved in the incident, the demands and opportunities are very different according to whether they are:

i) being interrogated by the police
ii) talking among themselves after the event
iii) having to explain to their parents what happened, or
iv) being confronted by the ghost of their dead friend.

Notes

1   I am indebted to David Eccles for this transcript.
2   From an account of work by Tom Stabler in Connie and Harold Rosen (1973).

12

JOURNAL SIX:
FATHER AND DAUGHTER

Protection and risk in drama

- engaging people in drama at a feeling level without them feeling threatened or exposed
- some protection devices: external focus of attention; tasks that create distance; choosing an appropriate viewpoint

Use of 'presentation' in drama

- strategies that allow 'actors' and 'audience' to collaborate in a common task of 'trying to understand and investigate'

Demands of working with older pupils

Had an interesting session the other day with my fourth year group (set 6 out of seven sets). I'd tried to use drama in various ways with them – none with much success. I'd tried topics with a greater emphasis on social realism than with younger groups – but it's not just the topics that need to be different with these kids. Strategies that often seem to get first and second years quite seriously committed to a drama often just don't work with older students. They are generally more suspicious and have a strong concern for their own image and a strong sense of others watching them. They don't want to take risks for fear of appearing ridiculous, and will respond to anything that seems likely to put them at risk by outright refusal, outrageous behaviour, or sullen withdrawal. Set 6 are particularly prone to sullen withdrawal – except for a small group of forthright and confident girls they are a suspicious and watchful lot. They'll get on with many conventional classroom tasks without too much complaint, but anything out of the ordinary and their guard is up.

The session I'm referring to was based on the following imagined situation:

> A girl of 15 is living at home with her father. Mother left the home a year or more ago, and since then the girl has been expected to take over the domestic work. There are considerable tensions between father and daughter. The girl presented severe behavioural problems at school and generally might be considered to be in some sense 'at risk'.

I chose it because it tied in to some extent with a short story we'd read recently. I wanted to approach it in a way that seemed fairly ordinary – much like a discussion (although discussion sessions as such aren't easy with this class!). So I said I would like them to 'be' a group of social workers discussing how they might help the family. I envisaged it going roughly like this:

Stage 1: On the basis of a written report I'd prepared, we would discuss the case – what further information we needed; what possible action we might take to help the situation. Though they would be asked in a broad sort of way to take up another viewpoint, that of a professional 'helper', no 'acting' would be involved.

Stage 2: We would interview the girl and her father, and possibly other members of the family or friends (if this seemed appropriate, arising out of the first two interviews). I thought I would probably have to be the father, but was confident of finding a volunteer to represent the girl.

I hadn't much of an idea of where things might go beyond this – I didn't envisage we'd get any further this lesson (a double period).

The material took off like a lead balloon. The class just withdrew inside themselves. I tried all the questioning skills I could muster – the best I could get were sporadic comments from Sharon and Jackie.

Afterwards I asked myself why. Was it that because some had been on the 'receiving end' of social work, they found the viewpoint I was asking them to adopt alien and distasteful? Was it that the social work 'frame' had trapped me into using, both in the report and in my spoken comments a kind of 'case' vocabulary which was offputting to them? I think one of the general reasons for this group's inarticulacy at school is that, on the whole, school presents them with a very different model of language from their own, and they don't talk much because they feel their style of talk is unacceptable. Perhaps my role language made them feel, 'we can't match that'. The social work frame was intended to help them to feel they could offer comments really as themselves, but overtly as someone else. A kind of protection from 'exposure'. But it didn't seem to work like that. It froze, instead of releasing, them.

Was it that the material itself was uninteresting? I don't think so, judging by what followed, but maybe the form of a written report to give the initial information made it appear so for these kids who don't find reading easy or natural.

At the time I was asking myself WHAT NEXT? Do I just abandon the material and turn to some other activity? Do I try to approach it in a different way? If so, what? An idea came to me. Without thinking much about it – there wasn't time – I gave it a try.

'I wonder if we could take a look at the kind of things that are happening in this family?' Dropping the 'social worker viewpoint', I was going to try inviting the class to decide what kind of events or scenes in the home they thought would probably go on – and then seek a few volunteers to play these scenes basically to the instructions of the rest. There were two or three girls who'd be confident enough to cope, and I could take a role or roles as necessary. It was necessary. I became the dad, playing a series of short scenes with the daughter, a social worker, a concerned relation (the girl's aunt – on her mother's side), played by the girls I'd expected to offer. It wasn't teacher acting to entertain the class – I and the volunteer girls were representing the characters and situations the class said they would like to see and the way they said they thought these might unfold. Obviously, in the playing, things came up that weren't part of our brief, but this spontaneous quality seemed to add something for the watchers, who were quite absorbed by the scenes, and now much more ready to offer comment on the action and instruction to the players. Not everyone spoke, but even the silent rump of half a dozen seemed quietly intent on what was going on.

The series of short scenes showed the tensions between father and daughter; attempts by aunt and social worker to intervene; the row in which the girl told her father she was pregnant, and after which she left home; and finally the girl's visit to her father, nearly a year later (her first visit since leaving) bringing the baby with her. This final scene was remarkable. Jackie played the girl on this occasion and definitely led the role-play, feeding me (as the father) all the time. Jackie is a very acute and perceptive kid – but I'd never quite realized how much so till now.

The scene began when the father opened the door to a knock. I then stood and looked at Jackie, waiting. She avoided eye contact but said,

'I've brought the baby. Thought you might like to see him. Shall I get him from the pram?' The bond between father and daughter; the huge chasm between them; the wish to make a move to heal the breach; the sense of its impossibility and of the need to guard oneself in making the move – all this was there in Jackie's laconic opening remarks and action. The scene that followed maintained and developed this ambivalence. Conversation was sporadic, terse, clichéd: 'He's a big baby, isn't he?'; 'Yes thanks, I'm getting on fine'. The daughter made the tea – they manœuvred to avoid hurting each other and to ward off intimate contact.

After the lesson, when I tried to make sense for myself of what had happened, I had a number of fairly incoherent thoughts:

1 There were quite a lot of occasions during the observed role-plays when laughter broke out at something one of the actors had said or done – it wasn't a destructive laughter, though, and each time it passed quickly and the group became quite serious and absorbed again. Thinking of this and other lessons, I think kids of this age, with their anxiety about committing themselves and their strong sense of the ridiculous, probably *need to laugh quite frequently*, and to seem to 'debunk' the work, because laughter releases tension and frees them to be serious about the work once the joke is over. So I guess it's probably important to accept, even foster, an 'in and out' attitude from many kids in the top end of the secondary school.

2 My playing a role, with the group (or most of them) observing, seemed to be quite productive. I suppose it showed that 'Sir' was willing to 'expose himself' and work in role/at risk. So I wasn't asking anything of them I wasn't prepared to do myself. It took the pressure off them (or most of them); attention was on me and the volunteer role-player – although the rest were contributing by shaping up, and commenting on, our scenes.

That contribution also, I think, helped the actors to be less exposed – they weren't so much presenting their own work to others, as trying to embody a brief the watchers had given them.

3 This session was different from any I've tackled before because the element of 'presentation' was much more central than in anything else I've done. But it wasn't presentation of the kind I used to think was what went on in drama: get into groups; invent and rehearse a 'scene'; come back and show it. Two key differences came to my mind.

   a) In this lesson 'actors' and 'audience' were *collaborating* in a way they don't in the other kind of presentation – so that they weren't really actors and audience in the usual sense.

   b) The purpose was different from the other kind of presentation – it wasn't to watch a scene others had devised, or to present to others a scene you had devised. Rather, it was to *understand, to make sense of what was going on* in the fictional relationship under scrutiny. That shared purpose was what enabled the collaboration between presenters and watchers to take place.

I had a long talk with Maggie – or more accurately a succession of snatched and interrupted conversations over a week or so – about my lesson with the fourth year and my thoughts about it. I've come away, I think, with

a) a clearer sense of what was going on in the lesson;

b) a multiplicity of ways in which I could have approached the same material and can approach other material in future; and

c) some general ideas which have taken my thinking about drama work on quite considerably.

Being in a drama demands to some degree an engagement of our feelings with the subject matter, theme or situation. That entails risk. Any situation which involves too much risk tends to produce withdrawal. We need securities to venture out from and return to. So in a drama which invites engagement of our feelings we need 'protection' for our feelings – we need to feel comfortable, secure enough to take a bit of a risk without feeling exposed, embarrassed or ridiculous. Part of the teacher's job seems to be to provide the right balance of protection and risk for the class. The problem is that the balance constantly changes according to the age-group (fourth years probably need more protection – or a different kind of protection – from first years); the class (amount of experience of drama probably counts a lot here); the topic (some topics have a greater emotional intensity than others, e.g. ones dealing with death or the supernatural) or the stage of the drama (a great deal of protection might be necessary early on, but once the class have become committed to the material they can cope with greater demands on their feelings). There seem to be a number of ways in which protection can be provided.

1 *By taking the group's attention away from itself and its own behaviour, by providing another focus of attention which is 'outside' themselves – which is 'other'.* This can be lots of things, for example a document, picture, or map to examine, or something similar they have to write or draw. I hadn't thought about it like this, but my written 'case report' could have functioned in this way – except it wasn't an appropriate protection device for these circumstances. A better one might have been two photographs, one each of father and daughter, accompanied by a verbal report from me as they examined the photos, or perhaps just by brief 'quoted' statements from the two, expressing their feelings about their situation. Then I could have invited the class to speculate about the situation and relationship, and so build the case history.

Teacher in role can be an 'other', a protection device. If I had begun the lesson by role-playing a concerned relation who had come to ask for advice about how best to help father and daughter, much of the focus of attention would have been on me: for quite a time the group would only have had to listen, or

ask questions. I could have brought the photos along too –
double protection!

2   *By providing a task which concentrates overtly on 'external
matters', while still moving into feeling engagement – but in a
way that somehow distances the feeling and makes it easier to
handle.* I'd never thought about it this way, but one of Maggie's
sample 'ways in' to a 'Wagon Train' drama – repairing your
boots and tending sore feet – is a simple example of this (see
p. 35). The overt focus of attention is on your boots and feet
rather than on the emotional issue of 'how much longer can we
go on?' This outside focus does, however, move you towards
that question, while at the same time offering the protection of
a physical task to concentrate on. So I can see how participants
in a drama can be protected into engagement of feeling via a
physical task or external focus of attention.

Another way of providing an external focus of attention is by
moving into 'showing', or more particularly into stylized forms
of representation – such as still image. Such a form can be set up
in a deliberate, objective, almost technical manner, and yet
make a powerful feeling statement. Again, another of Maggie's
'ways in' to 'Wagon Train' is a good example – the still image
of the burial of the baby, Mary Ellis (see pp. 35–6). The focus
of attention is on constructing a picture, not on feeling a deep
feeling. The initial and central figures in the image, the Ellis
family, are given their positions by the others, so there is a
double protection going on here: the people who represent the
family don't have to 'express' anything – they simply place
themselves as the rest tell them. The rest are constructing a
statement with a strong feeling impact, but employing other
people's bodies and a disciplined theatre form to do it. (To
some degree this 'double protection' was present in my lesson
with the fourth years – where 'actors' played a scene according
to the brief given them by the 'audience'.) Then the rest of the
class are asked to make a more direct personal commitment by
placing themselves in the picture in relation to the Ellis family –

but still within a form whose restrictions apparently 'distance' feeling. The next form is the soliloquy, which pushes them into an even more direct engagement, yet still through a clear and deliberate procedure or form.

I can now see how I could have employed still image to offer a 'doubly protected' way in to my material about the father and daughter. After giving some brief initial information about the situation, then the two quotations, I might have asked the class to make a still image using two volunteers, or a volunteer and myself, to encapsulate their initial impression of the relationship between father and daughter, for example, 'So you think he never listens to anything she says? Well how could we show that by the way we place them?'

This brings me to a third way of providing protection in a drama.

3 *By framing the participants appropriately, i.e. endowing them with a specific viewpoint on, or relationship to, events in the drama, which offers protection because it enables them to deal more indirectly with emotive subject matter.*

Take for example, the idea of a boy who is terrified one night by something in an empty house reputed to be haunted. Here are a series of frames or viewpoints from which it could be handled, starting with the most direct engagement with the experience and becoming generally more indirect, more protected and more distanced:

1 the boy having the experience now. (Likely to produce embarrassed withdrawal or exhibitionist histrionics!)
2 the boy recounting what happened to his parents or to a friend
3 his parents recounting the boy's account of the experience to a doctor who has come to treat the boy for shock
4 the friends who accompany him to the house, but don't go in, and who are waiting outside now
5 his friends recounting events as they saw them to a policeman

6   a police team carrying out a *daylight* inspection of the house for 'forensic' evidence
7   the headteacher addressing school assembly to tell pupils of the boy's experience and warn everyone to keep away from the house
8   a reporter, collecting information for a story about the incident

Tackling a drama on this topic, one might well start with a frame towards the lower end of the list, and as the class became more committed to the work and capable of more direct feeling engagement with the topic, move upwards – though I can't see the first viewpoint ever being really manageable because the emotional intensity of such an experience is so great, that some distancing would always be necessary.

Thinking of my 'father and daughter' material, here are a number of ways I might have framed the class after the construction of the still image. They are in no particular order.

a) As themselves hotseating the father and daughter, in order to find out about the situation and relationship, and to suggest courses of action and remedies.
b) As voluntary workers/social workers being asked to help by a concerned relation or friend.
c) As a concerned relation who is acting as an ear or confidant to one or other of the two.
d) As a concerned relation trying to intervene directly in the situation.
e) As the mother, or other close relation, directly involved.

We could have worked in a very flexible way to explore the situation: going back in time to discover how things got like this; exploring how father and daughter relate to each other and to other people in a variety of situations; seeing how the logic of their relationship is likely to develop in the future; asking what kind of help they need, whether they can be helped, and who could give it. We could have moved through a range of frames – the class as themselves, as helpers, as people directly involved. Either I could have tried to judge what balance of risk and protection they were ready for, and what frame I should employ to achieve that at different stages, or I could have offered the class the choice of frame, asking questions such as:

> What do you think should happen next?
> Should the mother arrive when she hears her daughter is pregnant?
> Should a social worker pay a visit? Or a trusted neighbour?
> Or first do you want to have a chance to ask the two of them how they're feeling after that row they've just had?

I'm talking about framing the whole class in relation to father and daughter. How could I involve all of them in that? I can see a spectrum of ways to handle it:

1 A volunteer represents the chosen role/frame and 'plays the scene' with father and/or daughter, but first is briefed by the class (as in my lesson). In a sense the volunteer represents the rest of the class in role.

2 As in (1), with the additional dimension that at any time the players can stop the action of the role-play to seek help or advice on what they should do now. Or the teacher may stop the action at crucial or testing points to ask the same question on behalf of the players.

3 As in (1) or (2), with the additional dimension that any of the audience may stop the action at any time, by raising a hand, to offer comment or advice to a player, or to speak on behalf of the player by moving temporarily to stand behind them. This can easily move on to (4).

4 The whole class represents a role intervening in the drama, e.g. if it is the neighbour trying to help, any of them can speak for the neighbour.

What this piece of work and the talks with Maggie have made me realize is that, whatever the age group, *there is always a need for protection in drama* – for helping the class to engage with the feeling in the fictional situation, without feeling threatened. To some extent, without really understanding it, I've already been using protective devices.

In the *Dragon Slayer* work (Journal 1):

> the documents provided a strong external focus of attention;

> the framing of the children as museum staff indicated clearly that no 'acting' was needed, only the adoption of a viewpoint, which created a critical and distanced stance towards the material;

> the waxworks idea would have moved them into 'representing' the material in the documents in a stylized manner that still offered a great deal of security, and could have been a bridge, if I'd wanted to move that way, into a fuller, 'living-through' dramatic realization of the material. This could, if necessary, still have been as the museum staff 're-creating' the period from the evidence – or perhaps that overall framing might have dropped away if the security it provided, and the need for 'recording' or 'representing our understanding to the public', were no longer necessary or fruitful.

In the *Lord of the Flies* work (Journal 3):

> In the early stages the focus of attention was mainly on me in my role as the naval officer. It shifted *gradually* to the 'boys' who were under the interrogation;

> the fact that each boy was represented by a group, and that it was made clear they didn't need to 'act' the boy but only 'represent' him, in the sense of answering questions as they thought he would answer, provided a lot of security.

After the work with the fourth year I was struck by the amount of 'pressure' I'd been able to put on the class through role. What I wasn't then aware of were the elements of 'protection' that allowed me to exert the pressure.

13
DRAMA
AND EVALUATION

'Trying to record a drama lesson is a bit like trying to record a party', a teacher said to me not too long ago. She was engaged in work on a Special Study for an Advanced Diploma in Drama course, and it was important for her purposes to get recorded evidence on audiotape of the children's thinking, as revealed in their talk during drama lessons. She was seeking more exhaustive evidence for her evaluation than most of us normally have time for, but I think her phrase is worth borrowing and amending to use as a starting point here:

Trying to evaluate a drama is a bit like trying to evaluate a party

The drama lesson is a fluid and complex occasion, with a multiplicity of social interactions.
It is transient in the extreme; there is little if any end product to examine afterwards as a basis for reflection and evaluation.

The 'meanings' (opportunities for learning) of the occasion are at many different levels.

I have to admit that my comparison breaks down easily if pushed very far. I use it for one reason only: to point the fact that most people would feel able to 'evaluate' a party without too much self-doubt or anxiety and yet many teachers feel unable to evaluate a drama lesson. Admittedly there is perhaps rather more responsibility attached to evaluating a drama lesson than a party. I would argue however that *the basis of evaluating drama work in the classroom are those ordinary skills of reading human behaviour and interaction that we all employ constantly in our daily lives,* for occasions small and large, important and trivial. I stress this because I think understanding it can free teachers from incapacitating doubts about their abilities to evaluate drama work.

Of course these 'ordinary skills' need to be applied thoughtfully, and need to be extended. But there is no mystery about evaluating drama work – it is if you like a matter of rigorous common sense. What I hope to provide below is a framework of ideas that will assist teachers to apply this rigorous common sense.

Evaluation requires clarity about aims

Journal 2 examines some of the difficulties a teacher can get into when he doesn't know what he wants out of a lesson. Not being clear about your aims means you have no criteria by which to take decisions about the management and progress of a lesson. Or, put more simply, if you don't know your destination, how can you decide which route to take?

But the problems don't stop there. Once the lesson is over, how do you evaluate it? If you don't know your destination, you can't possibly know when or whether you've arrived!

I think it important that a teacher using drama has articulated clearly a few key aims. For example, two aims for the work described in Journal 1 might have been:

1 To introduce the class to a text in a way that made its 'distance' a virtue rather than a problem – so that it excited and intrigued, rather than alienating, them.
2 To help the class to examine the text in the form it was offered to them from a frame or viewpoint other than their own – one which allowed them to speculate and hypothesize about the meaning of the text, and to search for patterns and connections.

These aims give clear criteria by which to evaluate the outcomes of the work. Were the class intrigued and excited? Did they take on board the 'way of thinking' offered by the drama viewpoint? Did they search for pattern and connection? Did they speculate and hypothesize? How rigorously?

These criteria help the teacher to evaluate the strategies employed in the lesson. Did they help the aims to be achieved? Use of teacher-role and language, of physical materials, of time and space can all be examined according to these criteria. Did they help the class to become intrigued; to be serious about their role and task in the drama, and to 'interrogate' the text in the way the teacher intended?

Of course, some drama work is much more open-ended. It's more a case of dropping a stone into the water and seeing what ripples it occasions. The lesson outlined in Journal 5 is more open-ended in terms of negotiating the direction of the drama than that described in Journal 1, but it is still possible to specify clear aims.

In the lesson on *Beowulf*, the teacher wanted:

1 to experience working 'at risk' (an aim for the teacher);
2 to define a clear context and place some possible tensions in the drama, but thereafter to place a major responsibility for the direction of the drama with the class;
3 to help the class take on with seriousness roles which demanded a significant shift in their behaviour and language – to each other and to the teacher.

So once the lesson is over, he could ask himself:

> Did I allow myself to work at risk?
> What kinds of risk, and what kinds of decisions was I taking?
> Did the class take significant responsibility for the work?
> What kinds of responsibility? How did I structure to allow for their responsibility?
> Were the class serious and comfortable in their roles?
> Did their behaviour and language shift to a mode appropriate to the dramatic context?

Of course where work is open-ended to some degree, learning areas will *emerge* during the course of a lesson: for example 'standing up to authority' and 'helping people cope with major changes in their lives and circumstances' became important themes in this particular lesson. So in addition to those aims and learning areas laid down in advance, evaluation needs to take account of those which emerge or are decided upon during a lesson.

If one is to be clear about aims and evaluation one needs to be clear about what kinds of learning are possible in drama. It is to that question that we turn next.

What kinds of learning are possible in drama?

1	2	3	4	5
Content	Cognitive abilities developed	Form – using the medium	Social learning through group process	Autonomy and responsibility for own work
	Language abilities developed			

I find the above chart useful for thinking about what children can learn or may have learnt, through drama. Each column represents a distinct type of learning area – though there is considerable overlap and blurring at the edges. The categories of learning area are separated out here simply to point out the *range* of learning possible through drama. It seems to me that almost any piece of drama is going to offer opportunities for learning in all five columns. The numerical ordering has no significance in terms of order of importance – all five categories seem equally important to me, although at different times and in different circumstances some will be stressed more than others, according to the nature of the work, the interests of the class and the purposes of the teacher.

Column 1: CONTENT

A drama has to be *about* something. There are always possibilities for learning in the content of the drama. And the range of content it is possible to handle in drama is quite breathtaking! By the act of shared pretence, a class can 'step into' any situation, in any period or place.

Within a specific topic the 'content learning' can be of a very different order according to the aims, stage, or structuring of the project. Early in a 'Luddite project' with a group of top primary pupils there were two sessions where the children built up their roles as stockingers.

> From time to time we stopped the drama to find from books and pictures, information which the children felt they needed: how a stocking frame really worked, what the lace stockings looked like, how much basic commodities cost in relation to their earnings, what their cottages would look like. Five families emerged. . . . The location and geography of their cottages was established as was the routine of the stockinger's day. (Tucker, 1985, 37)

Here basically the content of the drama was *information* about the stocking industry in the early nineteenth century. The drama was being used to make sense of the information, to elaborate it and give it a context.

Later in the drama, the content was very different. The formal content was the same – the children were still stockingers. But, when asked if they would take the oath to be 'twisted in' to the Luddite cause, although some agreed, others did not. The village was split, and most of the families within it were divided too. The drama then explored, 'What do the Luddites do when they are required to smash their own frames? What would the non-Luddites do if members of their own family planned to destroy their livelihood?' (Tucker, 1985, 41). The content here was not historical information but *moral choice* – in a context where that choice had direct and serious consequences for yourself and others. The children recognized this:

'I felt like sitting on the fence. I could see everyone's point of view and it was hard to know what to do for the best – but you can't do nothing, can you?'

'You know, it's difficult when you feel that you have to do what is right, but it's against someone you care about.'

In terms of its content, the drama may be a problem-solving exercise, as in Journal 1, or an exploration of human relationships, as in Journal 6. The possibilities are legion. It is likely however that again and again drama work will move into the exploration of moral and social values, for drama is a process that 'celebrates and challenges the norms and values by which people live' (Watkins, 1981, 163).

Column 2: COGNITIVE AND LANGUAGE DEVELOPMENT

Whatever the content of a drama, it will require participants to exercise a variety of cognitive and language functions – and these offer a distinct and important kind of area of learning and, consequently, of evaluation. I suggested earlier (p. 125) that a drama can be constructed to create any kind of language demand on children; I would also say, any kind of thinking demand. I have 'lumped together' cognition and language in this evaluation column. Those more academically inclined might want to insist upon distinctions between the two, but in practice the tie-up between cognition and language seems to me to be extraordinarily close: thinking is formulated and revealed through the medium of language. The table on pp. 136–7 analyses language use in the classroom in terms that would be equally applicable if it were a table of cognitive functions – e.g. speculating, predicting, theorizing, imagining, evaluating.

Thinking in drama is allied to feeling. And the kind of 'feeling-thinking' provoked by drama is cognitively very rich. How we think about a situation or problem is very much affected by how we feel about it, and the emotional investment built in a drama can give a considerable spur to our thinking.

Column 3: FORM – USING THE MEDIUM

Obviously one of the key aims when working in drama is that *participants should get progressively better at working in the medium of drama itself.* Teachers often find this a difficult aim because it seems difficult to identify the 'skills' of working in drama. If they are to develop in using the medium of drama, pupils, like teachers, must grow to understand how the medium works and what its laws are, and learn to put them to use. (At this point I suggest that the reader turns to the summary of some of the 'laws' of drama on pp. 22–3.)

Here I propose to touch on some aspects of using the medium of drama in which one would be aiming that pupils develop, which would be included in any evaluation of pupils' use of 'form'.

I have described drama as a 'shared fiction' involving 'an agreement to pretend'. One requisite for this is that *participants take the pretence seriously.* This does not mean solemnity or humourlessness, only that within the fiction participants behave 'as if' it were real. It means that participants need to treat their own role and those adopted by others seriously. The ability to do this will grow over time. At first the teacher may have to insist on it firmly and frequently. Later, as pupils realize its necessity, any lapses are likely to meet pressure for seriousness from the class themselves. In the early stages of drama it may not be possible for fictional roles to be too dissonant from habitual social roles (for example 'tough' boys will find the expression of 'tender' or 'caring' feelings difficult or impossible) but as participants grow steadily more secure in drama they will be more willing to adopt roles further and further from their normal social functioning in the 'real' world, for example boys playing girls.

Part of the reason they are able to do this is that as they come to understand the distinction between self and role, they become more adept at operating the 'dual viewpoint' required in drama and more secure in deciding what part of their 'self' to risk in role. The capacity to operate the dual viewpoint – participant and spectator – is another crucial area for pupil development and teacher evaluation. When in role one must operate from the viewpoint, knowledge and experience that role demands. To do that one may have to suspend one's own viewpoint, knowledge and experience, or that acquired in another role in the same drama – although these will come into play later in the process of reflection, or through a subsequent switch of roles.

Take for example, the group of 11-year-olds who spent some time as the inhabitants of the fictional Welsh village of Tally-bont, elaborating the life of the village, and deciding how to try to revitalize their declining community. Consider what de-mands were made on them when they were framed as experts working for the Central Electricity Generating Board and asked to examine maps and plans related to the Tallybont Hydro-Electric Scheme, which involved damming the valley and flooding the village; then when they returned to their role as villagers, unaware of the 'Scheme', and were visited by the boss of a large construction company recruiting labour for a big project in the region, which it gradually became clear, was a dam across their valley (Neelands, 1984b).

A class (especially a younger class) being introduced to drama will often get excited, and carried away, by plot. Gradually the teacher needs to help them shift to an interest in *exploring a situation rather than developing a plot*. This is a shift that even very young children can make. Certainly the group of 7-year-olds had done so who, on being read the story of Noah, were intrigued to know what the 'wicked people' had been up to, to make God so angry as to flood the earth and wanted to make a drama to find out about it!

A class working in drama should become steadily more able to read and use 'drama sign' – by this I mean the elements of communication which drama employs to create meaning, particularly: movement and stillness, sound and silence. All the brief examples below show pupils working on the use of drama signing, working at 'getting it right':

  i) Still image discussed in Journal 6.
 ii) Working in small groups, the class experiment with ways of making 'the sound we will all hear from our huts when the monster enters our village at night'.
iii) A drama where a person thought to be dead returns. The teacher says, 'So we think everything will stop and there'll be a long silence? Right, you choose the moment that feels right to confront us, and then we'll have that long silence. I wonder how it will be broken, and by whom? Shall we try it and see?'
 iv) Class discussion in 'Ahab and Elijah' drama quoted in Chapter 11.

Sometimes the class works at deliberately making a drama statement as in (*i*) and (*ii*), or at improving the signing in a scene already tried, as in (*iv*); sometimes the signing is a matter of immediate and intuitive response, as in (*iii*). It will depend on the occasion and its needs whether the class attends explicitly to drama signing, or whether their signed responses are drawn out moment to moment by the demands of the ongoing role interaction. Whether attention to dramatic signing is explicit or implicit, the aim is always to 'make drama work' and the attention to signing is always in the context of the dramatic fiction and its meaning – there is no need for exercises in 'theatre skills'. You learn to use the medium of drama by *using* it, and, at appropriate times, by attending to *how* you are using it.

Tension is the 'engine' of drama. Some tensions are cruder and more obvious than others. A clear gauge of a class's development in drama is their capacity to respond to increasingly subtle or complex tensions. A class who once needed, 'The Bow Street Runners are coming!' later can deal with, 'Each day we search each others' faces, knowing that, though we are partners in crime and depend daily on one another's skills and loyalty, the day may come when one of us will save himself from the scaffold by betraying the rest.'

Column 4: SOCIAL LEARNING THROUGH THE GROUP PROCESS

Although the *content* of drama is often about social and moral understandings, the area I am examining here is different: it is *those skills, capacities and understandings which can be developed through the process of group interaction and collaboration which drama involves.*

I think the best way to explain this is by a detailed example: a two-day project with a group of upper primary children, at a drama centre, where the class teacher and I were teaching collaboratively. The class were not really a group, more a collection of individuals and small friendship groups; their attention span was very short; they did not listen to each other's ideas; a lot of their behaviour was individualistic, egocentric, loud, attention-seeking and 'centrifugal'. In short, they were very difficult to work with as a whole class, yet at the same time irresponsible and immature if they were asked to operate in small groups. We wanted to see if we could use the opportunity of an intensive two-day project to achieve a significant shift in this pattern of behaviour. The context we chose was that of an open market because it offered opportunities

1 for small groups (of two to three children) to exercise choice and build investment in their own bit of the drama – their own stall, buying and selling, etc.; and
2 for the whole class to build a sense of being a community – the fictional community – the fictional community of the market-place.

The work began by concentrating on (1) then moving through to (2) without losing sight of (1). A series of short, clear-cut, enjoyable tasks, often involving physical activity were set, for example setting up stalls in the early morning; creating a sound collage of market sounds; trying to persuade a doubtful customer to buy. Very strong insistence was placed on listening to *all* contributions in class discussions, on being serious in role and on care and attention to detail in the drama activities. The class were clearly enjoying the work, and, by and large, meeting the demands it made on them.

Once the 'life and activity' of the market was established, we began to work more at its 'meaning' for those who worked and shopped there. This phase included:

1 inviting the class to elaborate the geography and history of the market and the market town through discussion. A statue and a well were invented by the children, which quickly gave the market a 900-year history!
2 the fiction that a TV documentary was being made about the market-place: a 'camera' filmed the market-place in full swing, and every stallholder was interviewed 'to camera' about his/her work in the market, how long they had been there, how they felt about it, and whether it would be missed if, for any reason, it were to end.

Subsequently (on day two) the market-place was threatened. First hints and rumours, then actual news, of a proposed redevelopment came; petitions were raised; protests made; a public meeting held; and so on. The dual investment of belief and concern in individual stalls and in the market as a whole, so carefully built on day one, now resulted in a cohesiveness, a commitment and a patience very different from their 'normal' behaviour. The air was thick with shared celebration when finally the traders heard that the proposed redevelopment had been turned down by the town council. The class teacher commented how very different their behaviour was towards each other in break times and lunchtimes during the two-day project—they were playing together instead of 'getting at' each other. The togetherness of the drama had spilt over into the real world!

Now I don't want to exaggerate what was achieved, or suggest that such changes are easily come by. The intensive nature of the project and its special setting probably enabled us to make more rapid progress than might otherwise have been achieved. The change in behaviour might only have been a temporary phenomenon – that would depend on how what had been achieved was subsequently built upon. But the class had been for a while 'released' from their normal, distinctive behaviour (distinctive to themselves as individuals and as a social and learning community) and had experienced another way of functioning and being with each other.

I go into many classrooms and I think it probably true to say that *the area of learning most generally neglected in schools is this one of valuing the class group and other individuals within it; of attending to, respecting and learning to make use of, other people's ideas and behaviour.*

Column 5: AUTONOMY AND RESPONSIBILITY FOR ONE'S OWN WORK

Some people believe that you give young people autonomy by stepping back, by non-intervention. My own view is that autonomy is built more effectively by *positive intervention*. As young children grow and become more independent, they don't cease to need their parents' support or help – they grow out of needing certain kinds of support, and into needing others, and so on. Sensible parents give support always with a view to their children becoming more autonomous – that might mean offering choice, or it might mean not letting them make a decisions they are not yet ready for. I think the same basic model holds in the classroom. Autonomy is built steadily, progressively, step by step, in the context of a relationship between adult and young persons where both have rights and responsibilities (see p. 47), where there is a real kind of equality, although the teacher has longer horizons and the children will tend to be preoccupied with more immediate satisfactions and goals. In fact autonomy and responsibility are learnt in the context not just of a relationship between teacher and learner, but also and equally important between the community of learners. John Dewey wrote of education as 'a social enterprise in which all have an opportunity to contribute and to which all feel a responsibility' (1938, 71). He considered it the teacher's function to plan for and enable the necessary community life in the classroom.

Autonomy carries with it responsibility – it is both an opportunity and a demand. My experience is that pupils will respond, not always quickly, but eventually, when they understand that the teacher is sharing his/her thinking and purposes with them, is giving them significant choices, and expecting them to share responsibility for the success of the work.

Earlier I suggested that decisions need to be taken about a drama on a variety of fronts, including: context, theme/focus, grouping, form, procedures, plot, role allocation (p. 37). All of these are areas in which autonomy and responsibility can be built. In the early stages of drama work the teacher will have to insist on certain basic conditions of operating. Some that a teacher might want to establish are:

seriousness in role
listening to, and building on, other's contributions
willingness to work with a wide range of people in the class,
including mixed sex groupings

The basic conditions thus laid down are ones that *enable the work to succeed*. Yes they constrain, but they are like the constraints we submit to in a game – the rules that allow the game to excite and involve us. The teacher needs to explain and discuss the reasons for the conditions so that the class can understand them.

The more the class understand through experience and discussion what drama is about, how it works and what demands it makes, the more significant the areas of choice they can be given. I will illustrate this with regard to the question *what will the drama be about?*

1   If at the early stages of drama work, the teacher asks this question of a class, the result is likely to be a list like that on p. 52. It may be then that the teacher, having allowed the class to choose the context, makes the decisions about theme and focus – i.e. what the play is about at an inner level of meaning.

2   Later, s/he might push their thinking further by saying, 'OK, so we are doing a play about outlaws. Do we want it to be about: *how being an outlaw affects someone personally – how their life is changed when it happens?* or, *how their actions affect others – say their family and friends?* or *their victims?*' In other words, the class are being asked to make choices about the areas of human experience that they will explore using the context they have chosen. At first they may have difficulty in thinking about a drama in this way and they will need time to talk things through.

3   After some experience of drama the class should become aware of, and concerned with, the 'meaning-within-the action' and not merely the action, and will become much more at home with the idea of looking at how a context might be used to

explore a theme, and at keeping that theme in mind in deciding how the drama develops stage by stage.

Perhaps the most effective single way of building autonomy and responsibility in a class is by holding regular evaluative class discussions centring around questions such as:

Did that work well do you think?
What made it work or not?
How do we deal with this problem we've hit?
What was the best bit in the drama we've just completed?
What bit was hardest?
How do you think our drama has changed in the last month/ term/whatever?
What progress have we made in that period? In what ways are we better at drama?
What do we need to work at in the weeks ahead?

14

SOME RESOURCES

General 'practical' books for the teacher

Lambert, A. *et al.* (1976) *Drama Guidelines*. A short book with lots of helpful bits to get people started.

Linnell, R. (1982) *Approaching Classroom Drama*. An idiosyncratic, patchy but likeable and generally helpful guide for teachers.

Neelands, J. (1984a) *Making Sense of Drama*. An extremely helpful book to the teacher beginning to find his/her way in drama. It puts much of the thinking about drama over the last decade into a very accessible and readable form.

Manuals

O'Neill, C. and Lambert, A. (1982) *Drama Structures*. The best of the manuals, indeed the only one I'd recommend at all. It outlines various drama projects for the secondary school, and unlike other manuals outlines the thinking behind the activities. There is still the problem that the 'narrative' offered in the book is seductive and it's easy to get trapped into following the plan rather than bending it to suit needs and circumstances.

Going in deeper

Bolton, G. (1979) *Towards a Theory of Drama in Education.*
Bolton, G. (1984) *Drama as Education.*
Johnson, E. and O'Neill, C. (eds) (1984) *Dorothy Heathcote, Collected Writings on Education and Drama.*
Wagner, B. J. (1979) *Dorothy Heathcote: Drama as a Learning Medium.*

Drama associations

NATD (National Association for the Teaching of Drama) and NADECT (National Association for Drama in Education and Children's Theatre) both offer annual conferences and other gatherings and an in-house journal or magazine – NATD's is *Drama Broadsheet*, and NADECT's is *Outlook*. NATD also has local branches, which have their own meetings – there may be a branch near you. Details from: Maggie McNeill, Secretary, NATD, 30 Heathdene Road, London SW16 0PD; Sally Manser, Chairperson, NADECT, Monega Drama Centre, Monega Road, London E12.

London has its own drama association, London Drama, which publishes a magazine of the same name. Details from: Win Bayliss, ILEA drama and Tape Centre, Princeton Street, London WC1R 4AX.

Drama journals

2D covers all aspects of drama in education: articles, interviews, book reviews. Subscription details from *2D* Sales Office, AB Printers, 33 Cannock Street, Leicester LE4 7HR.

Resource packs

Indians and Pioneers: the American West (1985) is the first of a planned series of packs of materials and resource items for teaching drama. Photographs, maps, documents, ideas for making useful artefacts, etc. are included. These combine with a planning framework, flexible suggestions on how to use the materials in the classroom, and skeleton teaching structures that teachers can flesh out by using the resource materials in their own way. Details from: 2D Sales Office, AB Printers, 33 Cannock Street, Leicester LE4 7HR.

BIBLIOGRAPHY

Aiken, J. (1976) *Midnight is a Place*, Harmondsworth, Penguin.

Bailey, P. (1984) 'Not so Bard After All! Some approaches to Shakespeare', *2D*, Vol. 4, No. 1, Autumn.

Bolton, G. (1979) *Towards a Theory of Drama in Education*, London, Longman.

Bolton, G. (1984) *Drama as Education*, London, Longman.

Brennan, A. and Llewellyn, S. (1984) 'Past, Present and Protest', *2D*, Vol. 3, No. 3, Summer.

Carroll, J. (1983) 'Growing Language – Drama and Language Development in Special Schools', *Drama Broadsheet*, Vol. 2, No. 1, Autumn.

Darke, Marjorie (1978) *A Question of Courage*, London, Armada.

DES (1967) *Drama*, Education Survey 2, London, HMSO.

Dewey, J. (1938) *Experience and Education*, New York, Macmillan.

Donaldson, M. (1978) *Children's Minds*, London, Fontana.

Eccles, D. (1984) 'Wizard of Earthsea: a way in through drama', *2D*, Vol. 3, No. 3, Summer.

Elam, K. (1980) *The Semiotics of Theatre and Drama*, London, Methuen.

Felton, M., Little, G., Parsons, B. and Schaffner, M. (1984) *Drama, Language and Learning*, NADIE Paper No. 1, Australia, National Association for Drama in Education.

Fleming, M. (1982) 'Language Development and Drama' in Wootton, M. (1982).

Garfield, L. (1977) *Smith*, London, Kestrel Books.

Golding, W. (1954) *Lord of the Flies*, London, Faber.

Hargreaves, D. (1982) *The Challenge for the Comprehensive School. Culture, Curriculum and Community*, London, Routledge & Kegan Paul.

Jackson, D. (1982) *Continuity in Secondary English*, London, Methuen.

Jackson, D. (1983) *Encounters with Books*, London, Methuen.

Johnson, E. and O'Neill, C. (eds) (1984) *Dorothy Heathcote, Collected Writings on Education and Drama*, London, Hutchinson.

Lambert, A., Linnell, R., O'Neill, C. and Warr-Wood, J. (1976) *Drama Guidelines*, London, London Drama/Heinemann.

Langer, S. (1953) *Feeling and Form*, London, Routledge & Kegan Paul.

Linnell, R. (1982) *Approaching Classroom Drama*, London, Edward Arnold.

McGregor, L., Tait, M. and Robins, K. (1977) *Learning through Drama*, London, Heinemann/Schools Council.

Medway, P. (1980) *Finding a Language*, London, Writers and Readers Publishing Co-operative Society.

Moffett, J. (1968), *Teaching the Universe of Discourse*, Boston, Mass., Houghton Mifflin.

Neelands, J. (1984a) *Making Sense of Drama*, London, Heinemann/2D.

Neelands, J. (1984b) 'The Tallybont Project', *Drama Broadsheet*, Vol. 3, No. 1, Winter.

O'Neill, C. (1983) 'Role-Play and Text' *The English Magazine*, No. 11, Summer.

O'Neill, C. and Lambert, A. (1982) *Drama Structures*, London, Hutchinson.

Peim, N. and Elmer, G. (1984) 'Othello, a Drama Approach to "A" Level English', *2D*, Vol. 3, No. 3, Summer.

Protherough, R. (1983) *Encouraging Writing*, London, Methuen.

Rosen, C. and Rosen, H. (1973) *The Language of Primary School Children*, Harmondsworth, Penguin.

Sharp, D. (1980) *English at School: The Wood and the Trees*, Oxford, Pergamon.

Sutcliff, R. (1970) *Dragon Slayer*, Harmondsworth, Penguin.

Tucker, J. (1985) 'Drama and the Moral Dimension', *2D*, Vol. 5, No. 1, Autumn.

Wagner, B. J. (1979) *Dorothy Heathcote: Drama as a Learning Medium*, London, Hutchinson.

Watkins, B. (1981) *Drama and Education*, London, Batsford.

Way, B. (1967) *Development through Drama*, London, Longman.

Wilson, A. and Cockcroft, R. (n.d.) *Some Uses of Role-Play as an Approach to the Study of Fiction*, Wakefield Literature and Learning Project 8–14, Wakefield L.E.A.

Wootton, M. (ed.) (1982) *New Directions in Drama Teaching*, London, Heinemann.

INDEX

abstraction, orders of 73, 75
accent(s), assumed 32, 38
'acting' 40
'acting out' 66, 86
active response 67–8
actor/audience collaboration 146
age-groups 141–2, 147, 151
Ahab and Elijah drama 129–31, 161
Aiken, Joan 48
aims 24, 25, 33, 126–7, 132, 154–6
Allen, John 80
analogy 83–4
animating text 66
'as if' situations 113, 116, 117, 125, 126
Australian research project 133–7
autonomy 164–5

badger gassing drama 121–5

barriers to text 70–1
beginning 35
behaviour problems 32, 38–40
behaviour shifts 163–4
belief building 24, 51, 90, 137
Beowulf 9
Beowulf journal, the 105–15, 129, 155
books: barriers in 70–1; 'core' of 69–72; for teachers 168–9
Brennan, Andrew 85
Bullock Report 68

Carroll, J. 118
challenge 39, 127, 137
children: as active shapers of drama 49; as experts 7, 14; in role 100–1; using ideas of 24, 25
class group, learning to value 164
class readers 3, 21

classification, of topics and themes 52
classroom layout, in *Dragon Slayer* 12; *see also* physical layout
Cockcroft, Roy 116, 117
cognition, and language development 158–9
collaboration 146, 162
commitment 51, 52
comprehension exercises 18, 132
concreteness 127–8
conditions of operating 165–6
confrontation role 105
content and form 69
content learning 157
context 26–9, 44, 51–3, 93–4
contract 44, 47–51
conventions 55–6
'core' of books 69–72

dance 78
Darke, Marjorie 85
decision taking 36–8, 47
definition 41, 42, 43–7, 51
Dewey, John 165
direction 91, 104, 105–15
discussion 21–2, 36, 52–3, 102–3, 137, 142, 167
distance 148–9
Donaldson, Margaret 127
Dragon Slayer 9–12, 17, 18, 71
Dragon Slayer journal, the 7–18, 70–1, 132, 152, 154–5
drama: common ground with English 20–1; definitions of 19, 21; laws of 22–3; quality of 137–40; use of medium 159; use of word 93
drama associations 169
drama journals 169
drama lesson(s): evaluating 153–6; model of 41–3; types of 47–8
Drama Structures 25, 106, 107
'dual viewpoint' 160

Eccles, David 71, 84
elaboration 73, 75, 78
Elam, K. 78
emotion 36, 147; *see also* feeling(s)
emotive subject matter 149–50
enactment 86
engagement 146, 148
English: its common ground with drama 20–1; a definition of 19
English teachers, problems for 52
enquiry 41, 42, 43, 51
evaluation 153–6, 167
expectations 24, 40
exposure 141, 143, 145–6
expressive language 133, 134
external focus 148–9

'facts' 134
factual information 27
Father and Daughter journal 86, 141–52
feeling(s) 36, 134, 137, 146–7
'feeling-thinking' 159
fiction: difficulties in 69–72; relationship with drama 20, 21; *see also* narrative fiction
Fleming, Mike 128
focus 33–6, 55–6, 90, 137, 148–9
form, and content 69
framing 54, 82–3, 128–9, 143, 149–52

Garfield, Leon 92, 129
Golding, William 60

group interaction and social
    learning 162
'group role' 59, 61, 93
'group sculpture' 17
group work 21
grouping 55

Happy Lion, The 137–8
Hargreaves, David 21
'headlines', use of in journals 6
Heathcote, Dorothy 19, 20, 70
'hotseating' 55, 59, 60

I am a Camera 78
identification 67
identity building 29–31
'illumination by transfer' 72
individuality 21
information 35, 50
informational language 133,
    134
interaction, making sense of 127
interactional language 133
interrogation of text 68
irrelevance 50

Jackson, David 67, 68, 72
journal, device of the 2–5, 6

'Keeper of the Keys' 106

Lambert, A. 25, 28, 106
Langer, Suzanne 127
language: reflective awareness of
    128–9; relationship with
    drama and fiction 20, 21
language aims 132
language development: and
    cognition 159; in a new
    context 116–18, 125; in new
    role relationships 118–25;
    varieties of 132–7

language embedded in action
    131
language skills, practising
    125–6
language use: by children 113;
    in drama 125–6, 135–6; by
    teacher 8, 13, 138
language work opportunities 8,
    90, 105
laughter 145
laws of drama 22–3, 159
learning areas 54, 156–67
'life-like' quality of drama 78,
    79–80, 128
Llewellyn, Sue 85
Lord of the Flies 59, 72
Lord of the Flies journal 59–65,
    72, 82, 152
Luddite project 157–8

McGregor, L. 121
Mcnamara, John 127
map, using a 27, 34
mapping 70
market place project 163–4
Marx, Groucho 78–9
materials, selection of 8, 24, 34
Mayor of Casterbridge, The 70
meaning 139, 162, 163, 166
Medway, Peter 19, 20
meeting, using a 31–3, 34
Midnight is a Place 48
model of a drama lesson 41–3
modes of working 55–6
Moffett, James 73, 79

narrative fiction, and drama:
    differences 72–80; similarities
    67–8
narrative text: drama strategies
    for, classified 80–5; 'in
    parallel' with drama 59, 90,
    92

Neelands, J. 161

Old Testament project, *see* Ahab and Elijah drama
older pupils 141–2
O'Neill, C. 25, 28, 106
open-ended work 155–6
open questions 48
Oregon Trail, the 27–8
'other' 147

pair work 30, 35
'participant mode' 128
'permission' to resist in role 105, 109, 119–20
photograph, using a 26–7, 35
physical activity 36
physical layout 12, 31, 36, 138
planning 24, 29, 36–7
planning framework 53–8
play, drama as 25
playtext 5–6, 86–9
plot and situation 161
poetry 5
positive intervention 165
posters, using 27–9, 34
power shifts 120
'presentation' 13, 141, 146
pressure 59, 64, 132, 152
pretending 159–60
primary school children group project 162–4
Prince and Advisers role-play 118–19
protection 141, 143, 147–8, 151–2
Protherough, Robert 126
pupil relationships, shifts in 120–1, 124–5
pupils, *see* children

Question of Courage, A 85
questioning 49, 60–5

'reading between the lines' 75
reading skills 8, 18
real life, randomness in 78–9
'real social network' 120–1
'reality' of drama, the 125–7, 128
reflection 80, 128–9, 134, 137, 139
resistance in role 105, 109, 119–20
resource packs 170
response, *see* active response, shared responses
responsibility 39, 165–7
'responsive reading' 68
risk 141, 146–7
role: and self 160; as a strategy for narrative text 80–5; *see also* teacher in role
role motivation, defining 39
role-play, value of 91
role-tasks, setting up 40
Romeo and Juliet 87–9

selectivity 33–4
self, and role 160
self-generating aspects of drama 113
shared fiction 159
shared responses 76–7
Sharp, D. 76
sign 74, 77–9, 161–2
skills: in drama 159; in reading 8, 18
small group work 34, 138
Smith 92, 97, 98, 99, 129
Smith journal, the 56–7, 84, 90–104
social learning through group process 162–4
'solidary experiences' 21
soliloquy 35–6, 149
'spectator mode' 128

spectators, and actors 86
still images 8, 17, 35–6, 86, 98, 100, 149
stopping the drama, reasons for 114–15, 129
story, and drama 21; *see also* narrative fiction
strategies: for narrative text 80–5; for playtext 87–9
structure 25–6
subjective responses 134
surface reading 71
Sutcliff, Rosemary 9, 70

tableaux 86
Tallybont project 160–1
task-pressure 132
tasks, breakdown of 25
tavern raid role-play 129
teacher–children relationships 113–14, 117–18
teacher in role: and belief building 46–7; in *Beowulf* 106–7; in *Dragon Slayer* 14, 15; in Father and Daughter 144–5; functions of 7–8; in *Lord of the Flies* 59, 62, 63, 65; as model 40; as other 147; in *Smith* 90–1, 96–7, 98, 101–3; as a strategy 138–9; in Way West 31–2, 40
teachers: aims of 33; assumptions of 20, 21–2; books for 168–9; key questions for 4; as non-experts 49–50; in role, *see* teacher in role
tension(s) 53–4, 137, 162; in

Lord of the Flies 59, 62, 64; in *Smith* 96
themes 24, 54
time: in drama 104; in fiction 79–80
time to develop drama 135–8
topics 43–4
translation of art forms 72
Tucker, J. 157, 158

understanding playtext 86
understanding relationships 146

validity in drama 50
viewpoint 54, 74–7, 139–40, 160
violence, enacting 95
visual art forms, and fiction 72
visual material, using 26–9

wagon train theme, *see* Way West
Watkins, Brian 41, 158
waxworks 8, 17
Way, B. 21
'way in', drama as a 7
Way West journal, the 24–40
'web of meaning' 75–6
Wilson, Angela 116, 117
Wizard of Earthsea 84
'*Wizard of Earthsea*: a way in through drama' 71, 84
words-embedded-in-action 79, 111
'workspaces' 12, 13
writing in role 59–65
written task, a 29–30
written work in *Smith* 97–8